Quick Lit
Student Workbook

Study of Language Arts: The Short Story

Grades 9-12

Jamie Collins

Ready-to-go activities that teach fundamentals of reading, writing, and thinking for the 21st Century Learner

Contents

Story #4 – Monday Mother

Story #5 – The Lunch

Story #6 – The Auction

Story #7 – Far From Home

A Note to
Parents/Guardians/Instructors

My name is Jamie Collins and I have developed this companion workbook with a love of literature in mind. As a teacher and author, I revere the art of communication—of story telling, in particular as a cherished gift and privilege. Story is as they say, "As old as time," and there is no better time than now to embrace the lessons and truths that abide in the themes, settings, and characters inherent in the human story.

Why a study guide like this? In a world where everything is a swipe or post away, students can take the time to learn—on their own terms in a digital or print format; whether self-motivated or through guided study. Either way, the **Quick Lit Student Workbook** puts *them* in charge. The grade-level appropriate guides help to promote self-discipline, foster reflection, and nurture appreciation of literature at all levels of the secondary learning platform. The short stories (sold separately*) offer a variety of point of views, themes, and settings from which to enjoy and discover.

Now, more than ever it is a great time to learn and to explore the timeless tenants of language arts— out of the classroom—and into a 21st century world.

The benefits of this workbook will help your student to:
- Focus on key ideas and details of the text.
- Understand and analyze meaning through word choice and context clues.
- Identify the author's intent through point of view, tone, and imagery.
- Identify and interpret literary devices used in conveying story.
- Synthesize and evaluate a story's meaning as it applies to themselves and the world at large. And much more!

I do hope that your student will enjoy this learning journey and that you, too will find it easy and rewarding to champion. Having a supportive hand along the way can make all the difference. Feel free to dive in with them in the discovery and the wonder.

Warmest regards,

Jamie Collins

Quick Lit, the short story collection, can be purchased in digital and/or print format.
It is needed to complete the learning activities. Sold separately.

How to Use
This Guide

There are 3 sections to each story lesson, starting with **Ready**, **Set**, and then **Go!**

In the **Ready** section, you will read the text first for enjoyment and then again for sharpening your close reading skills by identifying any literary devices, context clues for meaning, and/or specifics regarding story plot, setting, and characterization (to name a few). Be prepared to read and re-read the stories several times each.

Next, in the **Set** section, you will complete a series of assignments and quizzes that will help you to interact more deeply with the text by searching for patterns and clues in the story that you have noted, evident in the structure, language, and style.

Lastly, in the **Go!** section, you will have a chance to demonstrate what you have learned in a myriad of ways that demonstrate mastery of reading, comprehension, and written analysis along with other fun activities designed to best express your creativity and knowledge.

Dear Student,

For starters, the study of literature should not be difficult or a drudge. If you already love to read—great! If you ever dreamed about becoming an author and penning your own books, movie scripts, or video games—even more great! Understanding and appreciating the art of the story is a perfect place to start. It sharpens our minds, causes us to think, and even can open our hearts. Now, that is a wonderful thing!

I have crafted seven unique stories for you to dive into. Some might make you laugh; some might make your pulse race; some might make you cry, or cause you to wonder. Some might even help you see yourself and the world a little differently. Such is the power of the written word. That is its special magic.

And when you complete this journey to the last page, you just might be inspired in ways that you never imagined. Imagine that!

Enjoy…and happy reading and learning!

JC

Anticipation Guide

Think about the following statements and how they might apply to you or how you see others. Write a "T" for true or an "F" for false. *These are your opinions.*

_____ 1.   People are who they are basically from when they are young. A person does not change all that much into adulthood.

_____ 2.   A restless spirit can be tamed.

_____ 3.   A person should put their desires aside when it comes to God, country and/or family and make sacrifices for "the good of the whole."

_____ 4.   We owe our family and loved ones a debt of gratitude that supersedes our own needs and wants.

_____ 5.   Some traditions are to be held to at any cost.

Some responses may not have a clear True or False answer. Pick one that you feel is the most difficult to label either way. Explain why. Write your thoughts here:

READY: First Read

"Independence Day," is the story of a man who returns to his home town after being gone for several decades only to find himself haunted by more than just memories from his youth.

Read the story* through from beginning to end. You might wish to make some quick notes as you first read through the text the first time. Consider using a chart like the sample below in which to record your initial thoughts and impressions either while reading or after.

Model for the short story "Independence Day":

Events/Quotes:	Paragraph:	Observation/Reaction:
The narrator returns to the town he grew up in thirty years later.	5	*Why does he decide to come back after so long? Where was he living now? How did he manage to tell his dad that he was "leaving for good"?*
Joel and his dad talk about the horse that ran away.	30	*Is this significant? Why does Joel say, "You know what I'm trying to say, Paw?"*

Use the blank chart on the following page to add your own entries as you read through the short story. Feel free to make copies of it if you need more space to capture your notes.

Quick Lit – A Collection of Short Stories (sold separately).

First Read Note Chart

Events/Quotes:	Paragraph:	Observation/Reaction:

SET: Second Read

Now it's time to read the story through again, this time, paying special attention to some of the techniques used by the author such as **literary devices** that you recognize (i.e., imagery, dialect, personification and the like). Hint: Look for something you didn't notice the first time. Ask yourself, *how does the author use language and craft in a way that makes me see the story clearly?*

Tip: You may choose instead to make your notations directly in the book* along the margins, or on sticky notes. Or, you can create a notebook or "journal" to fill out as you read. Of course, you can use the chart like the one below to help you keep track of the order of events, the setting, the tone, and/or any other literary techniques. Be sure to include any questions you might have about a character or any concepts or themes you notice or wonder about. See pages 131-134 for definitions of Literary Terms.

Model for the short story "Independence Day":

Events/Quotes:	Paragraph	Observation/Reaction:
He describes the town fondly, remembering "walking her dusty roads and tossing pebbles into shallow creeks…" as a boy.	6	*He refers to the town as "her"— personification; lot's of imagery here too. The mood seems nostalgic.*
"…and then expel the blue streams from his nostrils like a rickety old smoke stack."	19	*This is an example of a simile – the author is using "like" to make a comparison.* *I get the feeling that his father is a relic like the old, worn out town. They are similar. Might this be significant?*

Quick Lit – A Collection of Short Stories (sold separately).

7

Name: _____

Second Read Note Chart

Events/Quotes:	Paragraph:	Observation/Reaction:

Deciding to move away or start a new life should be a decision that one does not take lightly. It is best to weigh all the factors. One way to do this is to create a list of pros and cons. Imagine if you were Joel and had to think about both sides of making this life-altering decision. List some of the factors that he might have had to consider.

Pro

"Yes, it is a good idea for Joel to leave his home town for a new start."

Con

"No, Joel should stay and help his family; his obligation is to his roots"

1.

2.

3.

4.

5.

6.

1.

2.

3.

4.

5.

6.

Fill in the middle row of the chart with the appropriate literary term. (Note: Some terms are shown in more than one example). The key is listed below the second chart.

Quotation:	Literary Device:	Definition of term:
1. "It was a hot July evening, still and quiet except for an occasional breeze that rose and lingered about the house, which smelled of fried chicken that Mama made for supper."		The general feeling the author wants the *reader* to have. This is achieved through description, setting, dialogue, and/or word choice.
2. "It was really something to watch my father smoke. It was sheer poetry."		When ideas, actions, or objects are described in non-literal terms. A comparison of one thing to another.
3. "I watched him take a last long draw of his smoke, pause, and then expel the blue streams from his nostrils like a rickety old smoke stack."		A type of metaphor when an object, idea, character, action, etc. is compared to another thing using the words "like" or "as."
4. "He looked out beyond the front yard, past me, to where the dusk was painting the sky a violet and rosy hue and popped the tab of a Budweiser, tossing the ring into the bushes."		When a nonhuman or abstract concept is described as having human-like qualities or characteristics.
5. "He had a southern drawl that curled all his words into questions that often made even defensive sounding tones seem melodic."		A regional variety of language distinguished by features of vocabulary, grammar, and pronunciation.
6. "He didn't offer his beer to anyone. Ever."		The author or narrator's attitude toward the subject.

10

Quotation:	Literary Device:	Definition of term:
7. "The smell of the wet soil permeated my entire body."		A word or passage that appeals to the senses.
8. "Are ya'll comin' in, or what? It's gettin' dark. Pie's in the oven."		A regional variety of language distinguished by features of vocabulary, grammar, and pronunciation.
9. "I can remember coming home after curfew one night when I was fourteen or fifteen. I don't recall where I was or what I was doing, but when I approached the house every light was out."		An interruption in a narrative that depicts events that have already taken place.
10. "Franklin is beautiful, especially in the spring. I had spent a lot of time playing in the fields, growing up, walking her dusty roads and tossing pebbles into shallow creeks…"		When a nonhuman or abstract concept is described as having human-like qualities or characteristics.
11. "I swallowed hard and felt the burn in the back of my throat."		A word or passage that appeals to the senses.
12. "Ain't nothin' on four legs you can't talk into doing something. You always had a way with wild ones, Joel."		The use of informal language and slang.

Dialect   **Colloquialism**   **Mood**
Metaphor   **Flashback**   **Personification**
Sensory Detail   **Simile**   **Tone**

GO! — Short Answer

Refer to your charts and to the text directly when you answer the following questions below. You may need to read the story through another time or
two to locate key items:

1. What point of view is the story told in? How do you know?

2. Who is telling the story?

3. What is the name of the town? Where in the U.S. is it most likely? How do you know?

4. In what season does the main story take place? What is the evidence?

5. How long had it been since the narrator had been back to the town?

6. How old was the narrator when he confronted his father on the porch to tell him that he was leaving for good that one "hot July evening"? How do you know?

7. What is the name of the narrator's brother who died in Vietnam? How old was Joel when this happened?

8. The narrator also relays a vivid memory from his teenage years concerning his father. Recap here what he recalls. What does this tell you about what kind of man the narrator's father was?

9. The structure of this story is told in multiple timelines, presenting scenes that have previously taken place outside of the present action. What is this literary device called?

10. How does the ending of the story make you feel? What emotion might it evoke? What word or words come to mind?

GO! — Critical Thinking Questions

Reflect on the following questions regarding the story on a deeper level. Consider how the text helps you to think or wonder about the characters, their motivations, your own experiences and/or the world at large.

Write your reply to each question below in 3-5 full sentences. Remember to use proper grammar and punctuation:

1. The narrator refers to the "old" and "tired" faces of the locals in the town that was once "full of color" that was now "faded and gray." What does he mean when he says, "Years of strain and hardships, I suppose, had numbed their spiritless hearts that never even thought to want for something more"?

2. What is significant about when the narrator says, "Stoic farmers in barber's chairs would prophesize, 'The young people, they go, but watch… eventually they come back. Have to—it's tradition that holds you'"?

3. Re-read the exchange between Joel and his father on the porch. He [Joel] says, "Hating him made it easier to leave." What does he mean by this?

4. Joel does not get out of the car and speak to his father at the end of the story when he drives by the house and sees him sitting on the porch. Why do you think this is?

GO! — Critical Thinking Questions

Reflect on the following questions regarding the story on a deeper level. Consider how the text helps you to think or wonder about the characters, their motivations, your own experiences and/or the world at large.

Write your reply to each question below in 5-10 sentences. Remember to use proper grammar and punctuation:

1. That "hot July evening" on the porch, the narrator describes his father in detail noting his "leathery" skin, "working hands", and "tired" eyes that were like his, only a "grayer blue". Why do you think the author takes the time to have Joel notice these specific details about his father?

2. Joel's father had raised he and his brother Conrad "to believe in three things: to be hard working, God-fearing, and accepting" which Joel viewed as "settling". When Joel says, "This is where he failed us." What does he mean by this?

3. The narrator states that in the summer of his twenty-fifth birthday, he had made up his mind to leave and that tradition was "not enough reason to hold me" and that "I had to liberate myself." How does this statement relate to the title *Independence Day*?

4. In the closing, the narrator says, "I guess it was curiosity that pulled me back, not regret." Do you think that this is a fair statement considering the fact that so many decades had passed? Does anything in the text confirm that Joel had second thoughts or felt remorse?

Assessment: Writing Prompt*

Grades 9-10

In literature, the application of **sensory details** enables the author to bring the reader into the world created. Such details include sight, sound, touch, smell, and/or taste. Include 2-4 passages from the text to support your response. Remember to enclose the passages in quotation marks. Indicate the paragraph number (the citation) in parenthesis. Remember that sometimes, a sentence can be a new paragraph. Your paragraph response should be between 75-125 words.

Prompt: In a well-developed paragraph, discuss how the author paints a sensory-rich picture in a given scene by including various sensory descriptions that help convey effective details.

Example:

In the story, the narrator describes the flashback scene on the porch where he is trying to work up the courage to tell his father that he is leaving. He describes the time of day as being, "where the dusk was painting the sky a violet and rosy hue" (par. 20). He goes on later to say that night was falling and "it was getting cooler by the minute" (par. 36). When his father shouts at him to go, the narrator remembers how "the smell of wet soil permeated my entire body (par. 48) and "I swallowed hard and felt the burn in the back of my throat" (par. 54). These sensations were imprinted on his memory and recalled in vivid detail in the re-telling of the story.

*See Rubric for Writing Assignments at the end of this section.

Your Paragraph:

_____

_____

_____

_____

_____

_____

_____

_____

_____

_____

_____

_____

_____

_____

Assessment: Writing Prompt*

Grades 11-12

Theme is the main idea or an underlying meaning of a literary work. This can be either overtly or subtlety implied. Here, the concept of "tradition" is mentioned several times in the story.

Prompt: In a well-developed paragraph (125-150 words), discuss how the theme of *tradition* is noteworthy. Find the passages in which the narrator mentions this theme and explain what significance it has in the story. Include 4-5 passages from the text, properly cited, to support your response. Your paragraph response should be between 75-125 words.

Example:

In the opening, of the short story, "Independence Day," the narrator establishes that when he was growing up, the family always ate their meals together by saying, "It was tradition—Mama fussing over everybody's peas and corn, and Paw mechanically chewing" (par. 2). Here, his mother's actions are nurturing, whereby in contrast, his father is seen as someone less "human" and more robotic and detached. This supports the tension between father and son as seen throughout Joel's childhood and young adult years. Further, in the summer of Joel's twenty-fifth birthday, he had made the decision to leave, saying, "Tradition was certainly not enough to hold me" even though the "stoic farmers in barber's chairs" prophesized that "it's tradition that holds you" (par. 7- 9). In deciding to leave, he was not only breaking a family tradition, but in some way betraying the town as well. Regardless, in the end, it became necessary for Joel to break free and create his own traditions.

*See Rubric for Writing Assignments at the end of this section.

Your Paragraph:

_____

_____

_____

_____

_____

_____

_____

_____

_____

_____

_____

_____

_____

Rubric for Writing Assignments

Standard:	Max Points:	Student Score:
Focus on Topic (Main Idea) Main idea stands out and is supported by detailed information.	10	
Support for Topic In-text citations are included and typed correctly.	15	
Sentence Structure (Fluency)	10	
Verbs (Plot summary in present tense)	10	
Voice (Writer's style)	10	
Grammar, Spelling, Capitalization & Punctuation (Conventions)	15	
Commentary Quotes/references explained	15	
Organization Pacing/structure/transitions	15	

Feedback:

Total Points: _____

READY: First Read

"The Ribbon and the Ring," is a tension-filled story about a mother who has a frightening encounter on a sunny summer day with a stranger in her kitchen who teaches her a lesson she will never forget.

Read the story* through from beginning to end. You might wish to make some quick notes as you first read through the text the first time. Consider using a chart like the sample below in which to record your initial thoughts and impressions either while reading or after.

Model for the short story "The Ribbon and the Ring":

Events/Quotes:	Paragraph:	Observation/Reaction:
Margaret's "delicate" hands are submerged in very hot water; the air smells like breakfast and lemon dish soap.	1	*This seems a bit odd. It's like she is not real and this is a fairy tale.*
The mother is shown working with a greasy pan just over her toddler's head as he sits at her feet near the sink.	1	*Isn't this a bit dangerous? (Foreshadowing?).*

Use the blank chart on the following page to add your own entries as you read through the short story. Feel free to make copies of it if you need more space to capture your notes.

*Quick Lit – A Collection of Short Stories (sold separately).

First Read Note Chart

Events/Quotes:	Paragraph:	Observation/Reaction:

SET: Second Read

Now it's time to read the story through again, this time, paying special attention to some of the techniques used by the author such as **literary devices** that you recognize (i.e., imagery, dialect, personification and the like). Hint: Look for something you didn't notice the first time. Ask yourself, *how does the author use language and craft in a way that makes me see the story clearly?*

Tip: You may choose instead to make your notations directly in the book* along the margins, or on sticky notes. Or, you can create a notebook or "journal" to fill out as you read. Of course, you can use the chart like the one below to help you keep track of the order of events, the setting, the tone, and/or any other literary techniques. Be sure to include any questions you might have about a character or any concepts or themes you notice or wonder about. See pages 131-134 for definitions of Literary Terms.

Model for the short story "The Ribbon and the Ring":

Events/Quotes:	Paragraph	Observation/Reaction:
"Steam rose . . . scalding temperatures" "The air smelled of freshly cooked bacon . . . mixing with the sweet lemon scent of the dishwater."	1	*The author uses sensory details here that appeal to the sense of smell and touch.*
"He reveled in twisting and biting the nipple causing it to squish and pop in his mouth, much to his delight."	1	*This is an example of onomatopoeia – words that imitate the natural sounds of a thing.* *This baby is typically curious about things and uses his mouth to explore his world.*

Quick Lit – A Collection of Short Stories (sold separately).

Second Read Note Chart

Events/Quotes:	Paragraph:	Observation/Reaction:

Characterization is the way that an author develops a character's **personality** in a story. There are two main types of characterization: **direct,** in which the author makes direct comments about a character's personality, and **indirect**, where such information is revealed through a character's speech/thoughts/feelings or actions, or those of other characters about them.

Fill in the last boxes indicating whether the methods noted are either *direct* or *indirect* characterization: (The first one is done for you).

What the story says	What it tells me about him/her	Method of Characterization
1. Margaret Baxter loathed housework with a passion, though she dutifully stood before the gleaming stainless steel sink . . .	According to the narrator, Margaret dislikes housework, yet she still tended to her "duty" as a wife and mother.	Direct (Author's direct comment)
2. She smiled to herself, quite pleased. Babies were not all that difficult to handle, she reasoned.	Margaret thinks highly of her child-rearing abilities; she sees herself as a competent mother.	
3. "Ice water would be mighty fine ma'am, if you wouldn't mind" [Benny].	Benny's words indicate that he is a respectful man; friendly and working class.	
4. His hair was a cluster of unkempt curls fancying off in every direction hitting his shoulders, and his mouth drooped open slightly as if he needed to keep it that way in order to take in more air to breathe. [The stranger].	The stranger seems to be unkempt and a bit "off" in general appearance.	

27

Name: _____

The Ribbon and the Ring
Activity #12: Characterization Chart – (Cont.)
All Levels

5. [Kellan's] wide liquid blue eyes watched Margaret's every move.	The boy looks at his mother expectantly as she is the source of all things.	
6. His [the workman's] eyes turned soft.	The narrator's description indicates a change in mood in the man at that moment.	
7. She was despondent, rocking and stroking the boy's head . . .	The author directly states that the character is upset.	
8. "Why don't you put it back on your lovely hand where it belongs?"	Here, the workman comments on Margaret's "lovely hand", indicating how he sees her.	

Plot refers to a cause-and-effect sequence of events that make up a story. The order of a story is comprised of: **Exposition, Rising Action, Climax, Falling Action, and Resolution**. Trace the order of events in this story starting with the exposition, through the rising action and the falling action to the conclusion. (The climax is filled in for you):

5. CLIMAX
Margaret screams and launches the boy onto the table, pries his mouth open, searching for the ring, presumably lodged in his throat. She berates herself for being so senseless and stupid.

EXPOSITION & RISING ACTION	FALLING ACTION & CONCLUSION
1.	6.
2.	7.
3.	8.
4.	9.

GO! – Literary Terms Quiz

Multiple Choice. Identify the literary device(s) indicated in each passage:

1. The air smelled of freshly cooked bacon and hung like a cloud above the kitchen, filtering out into the yard, mixing with the sweet lemon scent of the dishwater.

    A). sensory detail   C). Both A and B
    B). simile   D). None of the Above

2. He wailed so loudly that even the construction noises were momentarily muffled by the resounding siren that boomed from his tiny throat, turning his blue eyes ablaze and his face and entire bald head the deepest shade of red.

    A). dialect   C). foreshadowing
    B). assonance   D). metaphor

3. Down went the empty bottle, discarded in exchange for the pretty gold ring that glimmered and glistened on the rose-colored ribbon.

    A). alliteration   C). symbolism
    B). repetition   D). oxymoron

4. The yard was strewn with timber and insulation panels, and the center of the once-plush lawn gaped open with its innards spilled with disregard onto the brick patio in large black heaps.

    A). pun   C). allegory
    B). personification   D). elegy

5. For a quick second, Margaret thought that he might have been slightly impeded, what with the way his eyes sort of stared at her blankly, glazed over like small opaque marbles—as if they had no light from within.

    A). alliteration   C). simile
    B). metaphor   D). diction

Name: _____

The Ribbon and the Ring
Activity #14: Literary Terms Quiz – (Cont.)
All levels

6. "Naw, no need. I seen from the yard out there when Junior got in a snit on account of you wantin' to take his bottle away to wash it up and all, and how you give him your ring on the string so he wouldn't catch on that you took the bottle in the first place."

      A). prologue   C). pun
      B). dialect   D). idiom

7. He paused, drew his hand from his pocket and placed the ring onto the table with a solid *click*.

      A). onomatopoeia   C). hyperbole
      B). conflict   D). symbol

8. Margaret bent over her son, clutching him in her arms like a limp rag doll as he wailed into her bosom, confused and shaken.

      A). consonance   C). simile
      B). metaphor   D). diction

GO! — Critical Thinking Questions

Reflect on the following questions regarding the story on a deeper level. Consider how the text helps you to think or wonder about the characters, their motivations, your own experiences and/or the world at large.

Write your reply to each question below in 3-5 full sentences. Remember to use proper grammar and punctuation:

1. What do you make of Margaret's disdain for the mess being made of her yard in paragraph seven? How does she feel about it? What does it suggest about the kind of person she might be? What type of characterization is this?

2. At one point, Margaret turns around and is startled to find the presence of a stranger standing in the center of her kitchen. What does this shift in plot and mood cause in the story? How does it make you feel?

3. The narrator states, "Margaret felt her body tense" yet she "folded her arms across her chest to conceal it" (par. 28). Why does she try to hide her apprehension from the intruder at this point? Is she successful? What is significant about the fact that the narrator mentions that, "She eyed the kitchen knives in the strainer, calculating the distance. She could reach one if she needed to. Maybe" (par. 29).

GO! — Critical Thinking Questions

Reflect on the following questions regarding the story on a deeper level. Consider how the text helps you to think or wonder about the characters, their motivations, your own experiences and/or the world at large.

Write your reply to each question below in 5-10 sentences. Remember to use proper grammar and punctuation:

1. Does the fact that Margaret does not immediately pick up her son from the floor when she first encounters the stranger in her kitchen seem out of line with her character? What about moments later when he says, "You shouldn't have done what you done"? (par. 22). Why might she continue to engage in conversation with him even though she obviously does not trust him?

2. What do you notice about the pacing of the narrative at the point that Margaret sees that Kellan had "managed to work through the ribbon, which was now dangling from his mouth" (par. 35). What techniques does the author use to convey heightened emotion and panic here? How does this contrast with the next paragraph in which Margaret confirms that he had not swallowed the ring?

3. After Margaret begs her son to forgive her for terrifying him, she looks up at the stranger. What can be deduced about her state of mind after noting that she sees that he had a "faint tinge of triumph…flickering about his peculiar pressed mouth"? (par. 38). What does she say and do? Do you empathize with her reaction? Why or why not?

Anticipation Guide

Read each statement provided. Indicate your opinion on each statement or topic by placing an *X* on the scale line on the left side of the chart. Then, once you have finished this story section, re-do the exercise on the right side to see if your opinions have changed. Be sure to justify your beliefs with a few words of explanation.

BEFORE	Statement to Consider	AFTER

BEFORE	Statement to Consider	AFTER
_____ strongly agree strongly disagree Justify your opinion:	You can tell a lot about a person by outward appearances.	_____ strongly agree strongly disagree Justify your opinion:
_____ strongly agree strongly disagree Justify your opinion:	Actions speak louder than words.	_____ strongly agree strongly disagree Justify your opinion:
_____ strongly agree strongly disagree Justify your opinion:	Poverty is a state of mind.	_____ strongly agree strongly disagree Justify your opinion:

"Communion Shoes"
Focus On: Vocabulary

Directions:

The following vocabulary words are found in the story. Understanding them will enhance your understanding as you read. Define each one **IN YOUR OWN WORDS** first. Indicate on the chart what context clue(s) you used to help you to determine the meaning. Then, as you read, use a dictionary if needed.

Word	Your definition:	Context Clue(s):
1. Mass		
2. Catholic		
3. Communion		
4. kneeler		
5. Mary Janes		
6. mortified		
7. congregation		
8. triumphantly		
9. pew		
10. procession		

READY: First Read

"Communion Shoes," is an allegoric story about a young girl who comes into her own, and faces a truth about herself, on the event of making her First Holy Communion.

Read the story* through from beginning to end. You might wish to make some quick notes as you first read through the text the first time. Consider using a chart like the sample below in which to record your initial thoughts and impressions either while reading or after.

Model for the short story "Communion Shoes":

Events/Quotes:	Paragraph:	Observation/Reaction:
"Irene's sister Martha wore the Mary Janes second, parading down the aisle on her Communion day, quite certain that she was the <u>cat's meow</u>."	2	*What does this expression mean? Is this an idiom?*
"She was poor, and nothing short of a miracle was going to change that, at least not now."	9	*Will she get a miracle in this situation?*

Use the blank chart on the following page to add your own entries as you read through the short story. Feel free to make copies of it if you need more space to capture your notes.

*Quick Lit – A Collection of Short Stories (sold separately).

First Read Note Chart

Events/Quotes:	Paragraph:	Observation/Reaction:

SET: Second Read

Now it's time to read the story through again, this time, paying special attention to some of the techniques used by the author such as **literary devices** that you recognize (i.e., imagery, dialect, personification and the like). Hint: Look for something you didn't notice the first time. Ask yourself, *how does the author use language and craft in a way that makes me see the story clearly?*

Tip: You may choose instead to make your notations directly in the book* along the margins, or on sticky notes. Or, you can create a notebook or "journal" to fill out as you read. Of course, you can use the chart like the one below to help you keep track of the order of events, the setting, the tone, and/or any other literary techniques. Be sure to include any questions you might have about a character or any concepts or themes you notice or wonder about. See pages 131-134 for definitions of Literary Terms.

Model for the short story "Communion Shoes":

Events/Quotes:	Paragraph	Observation/Reaction:
"They will just have to do" – Irene's mother's words were <u>Gospel</u>."	1	*This is a metaphor. Her mom's words = Gospel.*
"It moved about, dangling like a <u>loose tooth</u>, ready to be yanked…"	10	*This is a simile; use of "like" to describe the dangling shoe, comparing it to a loose tooth.*

*Quick Lit – A Collection of Short Stories (sold separately).

Second Read Note Chart

Events/Quotes:	Paragraph:	Observation/Reaction:

Mood Chart

Passage from the story:	Mood that is created:	How is the mood developed?
1. Irene sat frozen in her seat. Moments earlier, she discovered that the heel of her shoe came loose.	Tension. Annoyance. Fear.	Plot Elements & Word choice
2. The once bright gold buckle had tarnished, and the wide strap around the center was frayed and ratted. The toes turned slightly upward at the tips and were badly scuffed.		
3. How could she walk up the church aisle in three-time hand-me-down shoes that were falling apart by the second?		
4. The Mass seemed to proceed like a blur of sounds and mindless gestures, all leading up to the crucial moment when she would have to face the congregation.		

Directions: Mood is a literary element that evokes certain feelings in readers through words and descriptions. This can be achieved through: **Word choice**, **Plot elements**, **Sensory details**, **Imagery** and/or the author's **Tone**. In the boxes below, identify the kind of mood that is created and how the mood is developed in the story. The first one is done for you.

GO! — Short Answer

Refer to your charts and to the text directly when you answer the following questions below. You may need to read the story through another time or two to locate key items:

1. What point of view is the story told in? How do you know?

2. What is the setting? Does the author give any indication of time or location? When do you suppose this story takes place?

3. What is the main conflict in the story? Describe. Is it internal, external, or both?

4. Describe the condition of the shoes by the by the time they got handed down to Irene after her two older sisters had worn them.

5. Why couldn't Irene have worn a new pair of shoes for her First Communion?

6. What does Irene mean when she attests that "Everyone laughed and cried and sneezed just the same as she did. Didn't they?" (par. 6).

7. What would you say is the theme of this story?

GO! — Critical Thinking Questions

Reflect on the following questions regarding the story on a deeper level. Consider how the text helps you to think or wonder about the characters, their motivations, your own experiences and/or the world at large.

Write your reply to each question below in 3-5 full sentences. Remember to use proper grammar and punctuation:

1.   What is the "crushing truth" that Irene realizes as she is sitting there, thinking about her three-time hand-me-down shoes? (par. 9).

2.   Can you relate to Irene? Think of a time when you felt out of place, or different from other members in a group. How did you feel physically? Emotionally?

3.   What do you think about what Irene did in the end by not wearing the shoes at all? Could you see yourself doing such a thing? Why or why not?

GO! — Critical Thinking Questions

Reflect on the following questions regarding the story on a deeper level. Consider how the text helps you to think or wonder about the characters, their motivations, your own experiences and/or the world at large.

Write your reply to each question below in 5-10 sentences. Remember to use proper grammar and punctuation:

1. What is suggested by the description of the other children "—the boys in their dark Sunday suits with starched collars and black ties, and the girls, looking angelic in their frilly white dresses, jeweled veils, and dainty white gloves poised reverently in prayer" (par. 6)? How does this contrast with Irene and her worn-out Communion shoes?

2. What causes Irene to change her mind about her predicament? What does the author mean by saying that "she realized that being poor was far less a curse than a *choice*" (par. 13)?

3. What evidence is given in the story that indicates that Irene's disposition had changed? What is shown in her body language and in her own words that attests to her shift in mindset?

"Monday Mother"
Focus On: Vocabulary

Directions:
The following vocabulary words are found in the story. Understanding them will enhance your understanding as you read. Define each one **IN YOUR OWN WORDS** first. Indicate on the chart what context clue(s) you used to help you to determine the meaning. Then, as you read, use a dictionary if needed.

Word	Your definition:	Context Clue(s):
1. croissant		
2. supplements		
3. stock		
4. arboretum		
5. germane		
6. sushi		
7. aesthetic		
8. gingerly		
9. alley		
10. mangy		

READY: First Read

"Monday Mother," is a glimpse into the world of a couple raising a mid-life baby in the midst of prosperity and privilege; however, resulting in a warped reality that only designates one day a week to the task.

Read the story* through from beginning to end. You might wish to make some quick notes as you first read through the text the first time. Consider using a chart like the sample below in which to record your initial thoughts and impressions either while reading or after.

Model for the short story "Monday Mother":

Events/Quotes:	Paragraph:	Observation/Reaction:
"His voice floated from behind the newspaper."	5	*Why doesn't her husband look at her? Is this important?*
"He just loves this news program. Ever since I first introduced him to it, he won't eat breakfast without the morning crew of CNN".	9	*What? How could an eighteen-month-old be interested in a news program?*

Use the blank chart on the following page to add your own entries as you read through the short story. Feel free to make copies of it if you need more space to capture your notes.

*Quick Lit – A Collection of Short Stories (sold separately).

First Read Note Chart

Events/Quotes:	Paragraph:	Observation/Reaction:

SET: Second Read

Now it's time to read the story through again, this time, paying special attention to some of the techniques used by the author such as **literary devices** that you recognize (i.e., imagery, dialect, personification and the like). Hint: Look for something you didn't notice the first time. Ask yourself, *how does the author use language and craft in a way that makes me see the story clearly?*

Tip: You may choose instead to make your notations directly in the book* along the margins, or on sticky notes. Or, you can create a notebook or "journal" to fill out as you read. Of course, you can use the chart like the one below to help you keep track of the order of events, the setting, the tone, and/or any other literary techniques. Be sure to include any questions you might have about a character or any concepts or themes you notice or wonder about. See pages 131-134 for definitions of Literary Terms.

Model for the short story "Monday Mother":

Events/Quotes:	Paragraph	Observation/Reaction:
"He found the jam to be a bit too tart for his liking, although he scooped up seconds, licking his fingers clean of the sticky red goo."	1	*The author uses sensory details here that appeal to the sense of taste and touch.*
". . . watching the city melt, melt, melt in the soft April rain."	21	*This is imagery.* *The mood is calm and mesmerizing (repetition of words for effect).*

*Quick Lit – A Collection of Short Stories (sold separately).

Second Read Note Chart

Events/Quotes:	Paragraph:	Observation/Reaction:

Fill in the middle row of the chart with the appropriate literary term. (Note: Some terms are shown in more than one example). The key is listed below the second chart.

Quotation:	Literary Device:	Definition of term:
1. "He found the jam to be a bit too tart for his liking . . . ."		A word or passage that appeals to the senses.
2. "Louisa disappeared down the hall with Pierce clinging fast to her neck like a playful monkey."		A type of metaphor when an object, idea, character, action, etc. is compared to another thing using the words "like" or "as."
3. "The day was dismal and damp." "Watching the city melt, melt, melt in the soft April rain."		The general feeling the author wants the *reader* to have. This is achieved through description, setting, dialogue, and/or words.
4. "How was she to teach her son anything on such a dreadful day? What of a butterfly could Pierce experience from a picture book or flash card alone?"		The author or narrator's attitude toward the subject.
5. *"Snip, snip, snip."*		The process of creating a word(s) that phonetically imitates, resembles, or suggests the sound that it describes.
6. "His main concern was that she would be careful not to announce Adolph Hitler in the same respectful approving tone of voice as say, President Reagan."		A criticism of a person, behavior, belief, government, or society as expressed through humor, irony, and/or hyperbole.

Quotation:	Literary Device:	Definition of term:
7. "A gray hue hung over the city like a colorless blanket as the wind blew an occasional spray of mist from a transparent sky . . . ."		A type of metaphor when an object, idea, character, action, etc. is compared to another thing using the words "like" or "as."
8. ". . . to mix like watercolors with the rain, swirling into the gaping, thirsty sewers."		When a nonhuman or abstract concept is described as having human-like qualities or characteristics.
9. "The late afternoon sun was just beginning to break through the hazy sky, sending streams of pale-yellow sunlight to fall and splash onto the sidewalk and the street below."		Visually descriptive or figurative language that creates a visual representation of ideas in the mind.
10. "His blue eyes turned to saucers."		When ideas, actions, or objects are described in non-literal terms. A comparison of one thing to another.
11. "She carefully tapped the patch of water with the toe of her leather boot causing tiny rings to move across the surface."		A word or passage that appeals to the senses. [touch]
12. "Catherine loomed frightfully at the mangy beast that was inquisitively sniffing near a dumpster."		The general feeling the author wants the *reader* to have. This is achieved through description, setting, dialogue, and/or words.

Mood   **Onomatopoeia**   **Imagery**
Metaphor   **Personification**   **Satire**
Sensory Detail **Simile**   **Tone**

Character Traits

Characters can also be described as being either **round and dynamic**, or **flat and static**. A round character is complex and might change over the course of the story; a flat character is simple and one-sided with no development.

Directions: Fill in the chart below with your impressions of the character named.

Character: Type: How do you know?

1. Catherine	Flat/Static	Although Catherine appears to have a moment of change at the puddle, she reverts back to her regimented ways of childrearing at the end.
2. Leighton Sterling Westbury III		
3. Pierce		
4. Sales woman		
5. Louisa		

Journal Writing

Consider the following question. Write your thoughts in free form, meaning whatever comes to mind. Do not worry about censoring or making corrections.

Prompt: *Is everything working right in this family? Are everyone's needs being met? Why or why not? Do you think that Catherine's parenting style is good/healthy for her child?*

_____

_____

_____

_____

_____

_____

_____

_____

_____

_____

GO! — Short Answer

Refer to your charts and to the text directly when you answer the following questions below. You may need to read the story through another time or two to locate key items:

1.   What point of view is the story told in? How do you know?

2.   What is Catherine's profession?

3.   What observations can you make about her husband, Leighton Sterling Westbury III based on what is said and shown in the text?

4.   What assumptions can you make about the couple's relationship based on their exchange at breakfast? About the family in general? What are some clues?

5.   Why is Catherine upset that the day is not sunny and warm? Where did she want to take Pierce? Why?

Name: _____

Monday Mother
Activity #31: Short Answer – (Cont.)
All Levels

6. What were Thursday evenings reserved for? Provide evidence from the text, what is implied, and/or directly stated.

7. What does Pierce do when he sees the large puddle? What does Catherine do? Why does she spell out the word, P-u-d-d-l-e?

8. After Catherine takes Pierce to get his hair cut, and then to lunch, where do they go next? What does Pierce think about it? What is the evidence?

9. The last stop on Catherine and Pierce's outing is the jewelry store. Explain what happens there. Why does the saleswoman "glare in horror at the child"?

10. At precisely 4:30 p.m., Catherine and Pierce return home and Catherine immediately hands her son over to his nanny. What does Catherine say to Pierce before she heads upstairs to work?

Name: _____

GO! — Critical Thinking Questions

Reflect on the following questions regarding the story on a deeper level. Consider how the text helps you to think or wonder about the characters, their motivations, your own experiences and/or the world at large.

Write your reply to each question below in 3-5 full sentences. Remember to use proper grammar and punctuation:

1. When starting home, Catherine and Pierce encounter a dog darting into an alley. With pride and exuberance, Pierce says, "Doggie!" What happens next? What do you make of Catherine's response?

2. What is significant about when the narrator says, "Pierce watched as the German Shepherd darted off down the alley, spooked by the intrusion; still, a dog, nonetheless" (par. 52)?

3. What is the theme or universal truth in this story? What is the author's intent? In what way is the title, "Monday Mother" relevant?

GO! — Critical Thinking Questions

Reflect on the following questions regarding the story on a deeper level. Consider how the text helps you to think or wonder about the characters, their motivations, your own experiences and/or the world at large.

Write your reply to each question below in 3-5 full sentences. Remember to use proper grammar and punctuation:

1. What is Catherine's opinion of her husband? How do you know? What is significant about when he says that she looked "frazzled"?

2. What is ironic about Catherine pitying the sales woman, who responds in horror when Pierce is lifted onto the counter, for obviously not having any children of her own?

3. What would you consider to be the climax of the story? Why? How does the image of the nanny "clutching [Pierce] securely to her bosom as she turned away from the boy's mother" sit with you?

Anticipation Guide

Rate the following statements on a scale of 1-10 (with "10" being the most agreement). Keep these ratings in mind as you read the short story.

_____ 1.   People create their own happiness.

_____ 2.   Telling the truth, no matter how difficult, is the best course of action.

_____ 3.   Family loyalty should come before one's personal needs/wants.

_____ 4.   We are a product of our upbringing, for good or for bad.

_____ 5.   Children end up carrying their parent's mistake/burdens.

_____ 6.   At some point in life, the child becomes the parent.

_____ 7.   An adult son or daughter should support his/her parent's wishes, no matter what the outcome.

READY: First Read

"The Lunch," is a glimpse into the endearing and often complex relationship between a daughter and her incorrigible mother, demonstrating that the hard truth is best served with a side of unconditional love.

Read the story* through from beginning to end. You might wish to make some quick notes as you first read through the text the first time. Consider using a chart like the sample below in which to record your initial thoughts and impressions either while reading or after.

Model for the short story "The Lunch":

Events/Quotes:	Paragraph:	Observation/Reaction:
The narrator says that she was really looking forward to meeting with her mother for lunch—"this time, for a change."	2	*What does she mean by this? Why is today any different? I'm intrigued…*
The narrator says of the lunch, "The ritual was well staged."	3	*What does she mean by this? By using the words "ritual" and "well staged," it seems like this is a command performance or something.*

Use the blank chart on the following page to add your own entries as you read through the short story. Feel free to make copies of it if you need more space to capture your notes.

Quick Lit – A Collection of Short Stories (sold separately).

First Read Note Chart

Events/Quotes:	Paragraph:	Observation/Reaction:

SET: Second Read

Now it's time to read the story through again, this time, paying special attention to some of the techniques used by the author such as **literary devices** that you recognize (i.e., imagery, dialect, personification and the like). Hint: Look for something you didn't notice the first time. Ask yourself, *how does the author use language and craft in a way that makes me see the story clearly?*

Tip: You may choose instead to make your notations directly in the book* along the margins, or on sticky notes. Or, you can create a notebook or "journal" to fill out as you read. Of course, you can use the chart like the one below to help you keep track of the order of events, the setting, the tone, and/or any other literary techniques. Be sure to include any questions you might have about a character or any concepts or themes you notice or wonder about. See pages 131-134 for definitions of Literary Terms.

Model for the short story "The Lunch":

Events/Quotes:	Paragraph	Observation/Reaction:
"She smelled of wildflowers and cocoa butter, of Estee Lauder and salon-grade hairspray."	10	*Sensory details = smell.*
"She soured, her brows frowning."	12	*This is an example of personification, indicating by her facial expression that she is showing displeasure or disapproval.*

*Quick Lit – A Collection of Short Stories (sold separately).

Second Read Note Chart

Events/Quotes:	Paragraph:	Observation/Reaction:

Compare/Contrast

There are notable differences between the mother in this story, and the mother in the short story, "The Ribbon and the Ring," as well as some similarities, shown in each story. Use the diagram below to illustrate the ways in which the two women are both different and similar. The area that overlaps indicates their similarities.

Directions: Fill in the chart below using several descriptive words and phrases for each character. Save this to refer to for a future assignment.

Margaret Baxter
From "The Ribbon and the Ring"

Mother
From "The Lunch"

westernmotodrags.com

Characterization is the way an author develops characters in a story. This can be done in the following ways:

- Descriptions of a character's physical appearance
- A character's speech, thoughts, feelings, or actions
- The speech, thoughts, feelings, or actions of other characters
- The narrator's direct comments about a character

Directions: Fill in the chart below with your own findings from the story regarding the character of the Mother.

What the story says:	What it tells me about her:	Method of Characterization:
1. "There, Mother sat, looking as chic as ever in one of her Halston designs and that distinctive, contented look of satisfaction on her face from a blissful morning of shopping."	*She is fashion and brand-conscious and finds deep enjoyment in looking stylish; she loves to shop for clothes.*	Description of a character's physical appearance.
2. "Mother reacted like a spoiled child."	*She is prone to throwing a tantrum and is doing so. She will not be contented with reason.*	The narrator's direct comments.
3.		
4.		
5.		
6.		

GO! — Short Answer

Refer to your charts and to the text directly when you answer the following questions below. You may need to read the story through another time or two to locate key items:

1. What point of view is the story told in? How do you know?

2. What do we learn about the narrator in the opening first three paragraphs?

3. What is the setting of the story? What clues suggest this?

4. What is Lindsay's profession? What is the evidence?

5. What is the one thing that both mother and daughter agree on in regard to the lunch?

6. Lindsay feels "a pang" when her mother mentions the holidays. Why is this?

7. What does Lindsay mean when she says, "For the first time that entire hour, I was finally able to exhale."

8. What causes Lindsay's mother to become upset? How do you know that she is unhappy?

9. What is the climax in the scene? What indicators are there to support your answer?

10. After Lindsay says, "I think you'll live, Mother. I really do," she takes a sip of coffee, calling it a "bitter brew," which was "soothing and warm." How might this action reflect the overall theme of the story?

GO! — Critical Thinking Questions

Reflect on the following questions regarding the story on a deeper level. Consider how the text helps you to think or wonder about the characters, their motivations, your own experiences and/or the world at large.

Write your reply to each question below in 3-5 full sentences. Remember to use proper grammar and punctuation:

1. What does it suggest that Lindsay had to trek nearly twelve blocks to the middle of downtown during the city's busy lunch hour to meet her mother for the lunch? What does that say about Lindsay?

2. Is Lindsay out of her element in the restaurant that her mother chose? How do you know?

3. Once Lindsay tells her mother that she will not be attending Thanksgiving dinner that year, her mother begins to cry. Her tears are said to be the kind "that drain from a doll when you fill it with water and then tip its head back, and then upright again; the kind that flow from large lifeless eyes." What do you make of this metaphor?

GO! — Critical Thinking Questions

Reflect on the following questions regarding the story on a deeper level. Consider how the text helps you to think or wonder about the characters, their motivations, your own experiences and/or the world at large.

Write your reply to each question below in 5-10 sentences. Remember to use proper grammar and punctuation:

1. Lindsay tells her mother that she is managing just fine and is happy with her busy life. She withdraws a bit saying, "I knew that I looked plain next to her," and "[Her mother] never could understand why the same things in life did not make us both happy." Is this a realistic expectation?

2. After Lindsay stands up to her mother telling her that she has to stop thinking of life in terms of only what she wants, Lindsay says, "I found it difficult to look at her at that moment. I felt guilty and selfish, but, at the same time, strangely free. Liberated" What does she mean by this?

3. What do you think of the gesture at the end of the story in which Lindsay offers her mother a tissue to dry her tears, saying, "I don't think that I had ever experienced a moment when I ever loved her more"?

Assessment: Writing Prompt*

Grades 9-10

A common writing assignment is the **comparison/contrast paragraph** in which you will focus on the ways in which two characters, for example, are similar (by comparison) and/or different (by contrast) from one another. Refer to the Venn diagram in Activity #37 where you listed the differences in the two mothers in the two stories as well as the ways in which they shared some similarities.

Prompt: Using the model below, write a comparison/contrast paragraph about **Margaret Baxter** (from "The Ribbon and the Ring") and Lindsay's mother, **Mother** (from "The Lunch").

_____ and _____ have some similarities and

some differences. First, _____ and _____ are the

same because they both _____. Additionally, they

both_____. On the other hand, _____ and

_____ have some differences. First, _____

(is/has/does) _____, but _____(is

not/has not/does not) _____. Second, _____

(is/has/does) _____, although _____

(is not/has not/does not) _____. Clearly, _____ and

_____ have similarities and differences.

Your Paragraph:

_____

_____

_____

_____

_____

_____

_____

_____

_____

_____

_____

_____

_____

Assessment: Writing Prompt*

Grades 11-12

A common writing assignment is the **comparison/contrast paragraph** in which you will focus on the ways in which two characters, for example, are similar (by comparison) and/or different (by contrast) from one another. Refer to the Venn diagram in Activity #37 where you listed the differences in the two mothers in the two stories as well as the ways in which they shared some similarities.

Prompt: In a well-developed paragraph (125-150 words), compare and contrast the characters of **Margaret Baxter** (from "The Ribbon and the Ring") and Lindsay's mother, **Mother** (from "The Lunch"). Include 3-5 passages from the text, properly cited, to support your response. Refer to the rubric on page 76 for scoring.

Your Paragraph:

_____

_____

_____

_____

_____

_____

_____

_____

_____

_____

_____

_____

Rubric for Compare/Contrast Paragraph

Standard:	Max Points:	Student Score:
Paragraph Structure Contains a topic sentence, at least 3-5 passages from the text supporting the differences and similarities, and includes a concluding sentence.	30	
Sentence Structure All sentences are complete; written in correct subject-verb order (present tense); In-text citations are included and typed correctly.	25	
Use of Compare and Contrast Signal Words All signal words and transitions are used correctly and effectively to identify similarities and differences in a logical progression.	15	
Commentary & Voice Quotes and references are explained; writing "sounds like" the student.	15	
Conventions Proper use of spelling, punctuation, and grammar throughout.	15	

Feedback:

Total Points: _____

READY: First Read

"The Auction," is a satirical story about a pretentious group of society mavens who elect to hold a "unique" fundraiser that leaves one attendee holding the bag.

Read the story* through from beginning to end. You might wish to make some quick notes as you first read through the text the first time. Consider using a chart like the sample below in which to record your initial thoughts and impressions either while reading or after.

Model for the short story "The Auction":

Events/Quotes:	Paragraph:	Observation/Reaction:
". . . which was comprised of many of the community's grandest dames."	1	*What does "grand dames" mean? Isn't this an antiquated term?*
"Audrey Winthrop pitched the response triumphantly. 'Men.'"	24	*Why would these ladies want to auction men—for a children's charity? This seems questionable.*

Use the blank chart on the following page to add your own entries as you read through the short story. Feel free to make copies of it if you need more space to capture your notes.

Quick Lit – A Collection of Short Stories (sold separately).

First Read Note Chart

Events/Quotes:	Paragraph:	Observation/Reaction:

SET: Second Read

Now it's time to read the story through again, this time, paying special attention to some of the techniques used by the author such as **literary devices** that you recognize (i.e., imagery, dialect, personification and the like). Hint: Look for something you didn't notice the first time. Ask yourself, *how does the author use language and craft in a way that makes me see the story clearly?*

Tip: You may choose instead to make your notations directly in the book* along the margins, or on sticky notes. Or, you can create a notebook or "journal" to fill out as you read. Of course, you can use the chart like the one below to help you keep track of the order of events, the setting, the tone, and/or any other literary techniques. Be sure to include any questions you might have about a character or any concepts or themes you notice or wonder about. See pages 131-134 for definitions of Literary Terms.

Model for the short story "Independence Day":

Events/Quotes:	Paragraph	Observation/Reaction:
"Someone hissed, *shhhh!*"	4	*This is onomatopoeia – the formation of a word from a sound linked to what is named.*
". . . the lull of anticipation that hung over her constituents <u>like a cloud</u>."	13	*This is an example of a simile – the author is using "like" to make a comparison.*

*Quick Lit – A Collection of Short Stories (sold separately).

Second Read Note Chart

Events/Quotes:	Paragraph:	Observation/Reaction:

Irony Chart

Irony is the use of words that creates incongruity between what is expected and what occurs, typically for humorous effect. This can be defined as being **situational**, **verbal**, or **dramatic**.

Directions: Fill in the chart below with an explanation of the ironic elements listed and indicate the type of irony that is used.

Passage:	How or Why is this Ironic?	Type:
1. "The idea of having an auction for the annual fundraiser was voted upon by the Committee of Upstanding Citizens Dedicated to Youth—"	The term "upstanding" is spelled out in the title (CUCDY), which implies that the committee would adhere to only "wholesome" methods of fundraising.	Verbal
2. "You can bet I'll be the first one in line to start the bidding!"		
3. "What was being said in defense of human integrity?" and "I would expose them, I vowed…"		
4. "And, moreover, as the first lucky bidder of the evening—had inadvertently just purchased bachelor number one for thirty-five hundred dollars."		

GO! – Short Story Quiz

Multiple Choice. Identify the best answer(s) for each question.

1. These and so many other <u>munificent</u> and giving spirits; the crème de la crème as it were, working their acts of charity like angels of mercy." Using the context clues, what does *munificent* mean?

    A). generous   C). proud
    B). stingy   D). bold

2. "Put a sock in it, Hildie!" and "You can bet I'll be the first one in line to start the bidding!" This is an example of:

    A). ambiguity   C). conflict
    B). foreshadowing   D). irony

3. "A quick glance around the room indicated that something of real importance was about to happen; something spectacular." This passage is an example of:

    A). tone   C). mood
    B). point of view   D). cadence

4. "Spotlights skipped and danced across the darkened stage creating a frenzy of anticipation." This passage is an example of:

    A). conflict   C). imagery
    B). personification   D). alliteration

Name: _____

The Auction
Activity #47: Short Story Quiz – (Cont.)
All levels

5.   Who are the "dinosaurs of debauchery"?

      A). the bidders   C). the terminally ill children
      B). the bachelors   D). the members of the CUCDY

6.   What does the second narrator mean when she says, "I gracelessly climbed over twelve sets of knees to the end of the aisle . . . ." This indicates what in the plot?

      A). she was trying to leave without   C). her exit caused a commotion being
                                                  noticed
      B). several people were in her way   D). all of the above

7.   Understanding that the climax is the moment of greatest emotional tension in a story, where does the climax occur in this story?

      A). when Audrey announces the   C). there is no climax theme for the
                                                  fundraiser
      B). right after the exposition   D). at the end of the story

GO! — Short Answer

Refer to your charts and to the text directly when you answer the following questions below. You may need to read the story through another time or two to locate key items:

1. What is unique about the point of view is this story? How do you know?

2. Where is the meeting of the CUCDY being held? What are the clues?

3. Who are the "angels of mercy"? What are some of their names?

4. What is the business at hand being discussed at the committee meeting? What decision is made as a result?

5. The reporter, sitting in the crowd on the night of the auction, is clearly opposed to having such an event. What does she mean when she says, "It was shameless, this idea of likening men to mere cattle in a common market where auctioneers sang to the highest bidder"?

6. What happens when the reporter gets up early to leave?

GO! — Critical Thinking Questions

Reflect on the following questions regarding the story on a deeper level. Consider how the text helps you to think or wonder about the characters, their motivations, your own experiences and/or the world at large.

Write your reply to each question below in 3-5 full sentences. Remember to use proper grammar and punctuation:

1. There seems to be some old-fashioned elements in the story alongside some modern-day references. Can you find some examples? In what year do you suppose this story takes place? What clues make you think so and why?

2. What do you personally think about having an auction of this "sort" as a means to raise money for a good cause? Was this inappropriate seeing as how the charity in question was for terminally ill children?

GO! — Critical Thinking Questions

Reflect on the following questions regarding the story on a deeper level. Consider how the text helps you to think or wonder about the characters, their motivations, your own experiences and/or the world at large.

Write your reply to each question below in 3-5 full sentences. Remember to use proper grammar and punctuation:

1. Satire in stories and poems often utilizes humor, irony, exaggeration, and/or ridicule to expose shortcomings, follies, and vices. Can you identify some elements in this short story that employ satire?

2. What do you personally think about having an auction of this "sort" as a means to raise money for a good cause? Was this inappropriate seeing as how the charity in question was for terminally ill children? What might have been the author's purpose for writing this satire?

Name: _____

The Auction
Activity #51: Get Creative!
All Levels

GO! – Get Creative!

A fun part of the creative process is to imagine alternative endings to some of the stories we read. Ask yourself, *What if?* What if things went differently on the night of the bachelor auction? What would you write to give this satirical story a twist ending of your own? Go crazy! Let your imagination run wild!

Your alternative ending: (See Rubric for Writing Assignments at the end of this section).

_____

_____

_____

_____

_____

_____

_____

_____

_____

_____

_____

Name: _____

The Auction
Activity #51: Get Creative!
(Cont.)—All Levels

_____

_____

_____

_____

_____

_____

_____

_____

_____

_____

_____

_____

_____

_____

Name: _____

The Auction
Activity #51: Get Creative!
(Cont.)—All Levels

_____

_____

_____

_____

_____

_____

_____

_____

_____

_____

_____

_____

_____

_____

_____

Creative Writing Rubric

Standard:	Max Points:	Student Score:
Captures Attention The writing is interesting from the first sentence, paragraph, or line, enticing the reader to continue reading.	5	
Original Demonstrates original use of ideas, imagery, dialogue, plot, character development, etc. Language is fresh and unique to the writer's voice.	10	
Sustains Interest Succeeds in pulling the reader along with a desire to know "what's next" and works toward solving a problem with a satisfactory outcome for the reader.	10	
Clarity and Conclusion Leaves no room for uncertainty (unless intended); character motives and traits are clear and communicated well. The conclusion is defined.	10	
Conventions Proper use of spelling, punctuation, and grammar throughout. Use of language is optimized for an aesthetic effect.	15	

Feedback:

Total Points: _____

Name: _____

The Auction
Activity #51: Get Creative!
All Levels

GO! – Get Creative!

A picture is worth a thousand words. Draw a sketch of the character Audrey Winthrop following the descriptions given in the short story. Feel free to embellish or exaggerate her image as a caricature or cartoon.

Place your drawing in the frame below:

Anticipation Guide

Think about the following statements and how they might apply to you or how you see the topic. Write a "T" for true or an "F" for false. *These are your opinions.*

_____ 1.   Fighting for a cause always comes at a price.

_____ 2.   Sometimes "best intentions" can backfire.

_____ 3.   One person can make a difference.

_____ 4.   Bleeding hearts are foolish hearts.

_____ 5.   Freedom is a privilege and not guaranteed.

Some responses may not have a clear True or False answer. Pick one that you feel is the most difficult to label either way. Explain why. Write your thoughts here:

READY: First Read

"Far From Home," is the story of a professor who accompanies a group of college students on a missionary trip to Central America in the early 1980s, during the volatile turmoil of the Salvadoran Civil War.

Read the story* through from beginning to end. You might wish to make some quick notes as you first read through the text the first time. Consider using a chart like the sample below in which to record your initial thoughts and impressions either while reading or after.

Model for the short story "Far From Home":

Events/Quotes:	Paragraph:	Observation/Reaction:
The narrator indicates that he is a foreigner in a desolate place. It appears to be very hot there.	1	*This might be a third-world country; the boy is alone. Why is this?*
There is "burnt ash and gunpowder hanging in the air . . .."	2	*This signifies fighting or war.*

Use the blank chart on the following page to add your own entries as you read through the short story. Feel free to make copies of it if you need more space to capture your notes.

*Quick Lit – A Collection of Short Stories (sold separately).

First Read Note Chart

Events/Quotes:	Paragraph:	Observation/Reaction:

SET: Second Read

Now it's time to read the story through again, this time, paying special attention to some of the techniques used by the author such as **literary devices** that you recognize (i.e., imagery, dialect, personification and the like). Hint: Look for something you didn't notice the first time. Ask yourself, *how does the author use language and craft in a way that makes me see the story clearly?*

Tip: You may choose instead to make your notations directly in the book* along the margins, or on sticky notes. Or, you can create a notebook or "journal" to fill out as you read. Of course, you can use the chart like the one below to help you keep track of the order of events, the setting, the tone, and/or any other literary techniques. Be sure to include any questions you might have about a character or any concepts or themes you notice or wonder about. See pages 131-134 for definitions of Literary Terms.

Model for the short story "Far From Home":

Events/Quotes:	Paragraph	Observation/Reaction:
". . . Salvador's hot savage breath."	2	*This is an example of personification; the wind is compared to being the country's very breath.*
"Outside, the village slept silent under the peaceful shroud of the night sky."	46	*This is a metaphor; the night sky is said to be "blanketing" the sky over the village. Ironically, a <u>shroud</u> is a death cloth.*

Quick Lit – A Collection of Short Stories (sold separately).

Second Read Note Chart

Events/Quotes:	Paragraph:	Observation/Reaction:

Characterization Chart

Directions: Fill in the chart below with your findings about each character listed, taken directly from the text, giving an example for each method.

Character:	Speech/Actions/Thoughts of the Character	Speech/Actions/Thoughts of another Character about him/her
1. McLadd	"McLadd bounded into the room behind the others bare-chested and wearing nothing but his shorts and a pair of red high-tops. He was grinning like a fool."	"I ignored his pathetic attempt at humor and dismissed his behavior as being either recompense for my failing him fall term, or sheer ignorance, which was the more probable guess."
2. **Malcolm**		
3. **Eileen**		
4. **Nathan**		
5. **Michael Anne**		
6. **Dr. Johns**		
7. **Rosita**		
8. **Young boy**		

Imagery/Sensory Chart

Directions: Imagery is used to create a picture in the reader's mind. The author uses language that appeals to one or more of the five senses. Fill in examples from the story for each of the senses listed.

Sight	1. ". . . save for the dwarf spherical mass that burned fiercely—mercilessly."
Smell	2.
Hearing	3.
Taste	4.
Touch	5.

Conclusions Chart

Directions: Fill in the chart with conclusions inspired by the key events listed.

Section	Key Event	Make a Conclusion About:
Arrival	The narrator regrets not taking a photo of the boy he sees by the wagon wheel beneath the hot sun when he had the chance.	**1. Missed opportunities in life:**
Encounter	The boy is later seen with his brother, and older sister at the church service. The narrator comments about the girl, "it was faith that had brought her to God's house, not pride."	**2. The expectation in society for people's worth to be related to their means:**
Rosita's Kitchen	A gunshot is heard above the noisy kitchen chatter. Rosita's soulful eyes seem to ask why they had even come.	**3. The reasons for risking one's life to help others:**
Harvest	The narrator says that to this day, he "cannot drink a cup of coffee without images of that vast plantation tugging at the mind's eye."	**4. Appreciation for workers who provide for the many:**
One Night	"Only what was the separation? Fantasy from reality, life from death, bondage from freedom?"	**5. The concept of one's reality being tested by adversity:**
No Honor	Dr. Johns and his crew hand out school supplies to the children in need. It was like a "holiday."	**6. What small gestures mean in the bigger picture:**
Death	There, Rosita and her family stood, grieving the curses of a war that laid death at their door.	**7. Coping with death during a war:**
Awakening	"Oh, to have made a difference!"	**8. The human spirit's need to find meaning:**

GO! — Short Answer

Refer to your charts and to the text directly when you answer the following questions below. You may need to read the story through another time or two to locate key items:

1. What point of view is the story told in? How do you know?

2. Who is the narrator? Who else is with him on this trip? Why are they all there?

3. What are some clues from the text that help set up the sense of place or setting in the story? Give examples.

Name: _____

Far From Home
Activity #58: Short Answer - All Levels (Cont.)

4. How does the sensory element of oppressive heat contribute to the story? Provide some examples.

5. Why do you think the author divides each scene into separate sections? What effect does this add to the story?

6. Why is it ironic that the locals pick the coffee berries from bushes that look like "miniature" Christmas trees? What does the narrator mean when he says, "What of a holiday could these people know?"

7. How is the distribution of supplies from the States "a holiday after all"?

8. Before their departure, the group gathers at Rosita's house. What is the "sad and silent awkwardness" that is hanging in the air? What has happened to cause this?

GO! — Critical Thinking Questions

Reflect on the following questions regarding the story on a deeper level. Consider how the text helps you to think or wonder about the characters, their motivations, your own experiences and/or the world at large.

Write your reply to each question below in 3-5 full sentences. Remember to use proper grammar and punctuation:

1. The morning in Rosita's kitchen, when a sudden gunshot sounded, and "the soulful plea in her dark eyes seemed to ask why we had even come." The narrator says, "I was never quite certain if she had resented us being there." What do you think he means by this?

2. After distributing the school supplies to the children, the narrator looks at the "countless faces" around him, noting that they all have the same "marked desperateness" that he saw that first day in the boy near the wagon wheel. This causes "a feeling of remorse" to creep into his "once-elated" soul. What does he mean by this?

3. In the final scene, the narrator notes that "the light in Eileen's eyes had lessoned, and a stony coldness took its pace." Why is this so?

GO! — Critical Thinking Questions

Reflect on the following questions regarding the story on a deeper level. Consider how the text helps you to think or wonder about the characters, their motivations, your own experiences and/or the world at large.

Write your reply to each question below in 3-5 full sentences. Remember to use proper grammar and punctuation:

1. In the section "One Night," the narrator contemplates in the dark, during a quiet reprieve, about the purpose as to why he had come to Salvador. He asks, what is the "separation" of "Fantasy from reality, life from death, and bondage from freedom?" What does he mean here?

2. The same night, as a soft rumbling of gunfire is heard far off in the hills. He thinks about the young girl in the church with her siblings clinging to her with "wide frightened eyes." He listens to Eileen's muffled sobs as she lay weeping, and says, "I never felt so far from home." What does he mean by this?

3. In the final scene, the narrator expresses guilt that he had brought Eileen and the others to the "destruction and poverty" of a "senseless war" for answers that "did not exist." He never stops looking back at the village from that day forward. Why? Do you think he ever will?

Essay Writing Prompt*

Everyone has his or her own beliefs. While knowing where you stand on an issue may be easy for you to know, it might be a little more difficult to articulate to others, namely, in an essay format.

You will be writing a well-developed four (4) paragraph narrative essay in which you draw on a *personal experience* that relays your fundamental belief in an interesting and artistic way. Hand write or type this essay on a separate document.

Of course, keep these key components in mind:

- The essay should clearly articulate your central belief.
- The tone of your essay should fit your personality. Make sure that the voice is "yours." Write the narrative in first-person.
- The word count should be between 350-500 words.
- Incorporate the six traits of writing with attention to detail in all aspects of composition.
- Be sure to adhere to all conventions of correct punctuation and grammar.

Choose ONE prompt from the Anticipation Guide exercise from earlier in this section. Here they are again:

1. Fighting for a cause always comes at a price.

2. Sometimes "best intentions" can backfire.

3. One person can make a difference.

4. Bleeding hearts are foolish hearts.

5. Freedom is a privilege and not guaranteed.

*See Rubric for Writing Assignments at the end of this section.

Essay Writing Prompt*

Everyone has his or her own beliefs. While knowing where you stand on an issue may be easy for you to know, it might be a little more difficult to articulate to others, namely, in an essay format.

You will be writing a well-developed four (5-6) paragraph narrative essay in which you draw on a *personal experience* that relays your fundamental belief in an interesting and artistic way. Hand write or type this essay on a separate document.

Of course, keep these key components in mind:

- The essay should clearly articulate your central belief.
- The tone of your essay should fit your personality. Make sure that the voice is "yours." Write the narrative in first-person.
- The word count should be between 450-750 words.
- Incorporate the six traits of writing with attention to detail in all aspects of composition.
- Be sure to adhere to all conventions of correct punctuation and grammar.

Choose ONE prompt from the Anticipation Guide exercise from earlier in this section. Here they are again:

1. Fighting for a cause always comes at a price.

2. Sometimes "best intentions" can backfire.

3. One person can make a difference.

4. Bleeding hearts are foolish hearts.

5. Freedom is a privilege and not guaranteed.

*See Rubric for Writing Assignments at the end of this section.

"Tips" for Drafting an Effective Personal Narrative

Start your narrative strong.
Your HOOK is the most important part of the entire passage; it is what will draw your reader in and keep him or her interested in your story. Leading with, "I'm going to tell you about a time I felt nervous at a dance recital," is not an adequate start. Use something like "I could feel my palms begin to sweat and my knees grow weak; I knew that I should have practiced more before the big night" instead. Try to grab the reader's interest right from the first sentence.

Use dialogue in your narrative.
It is remarkable how much we learn about people from what they say. One way to achieve this is through carefully written—and realistic, dialogue. Work to draft dialogue that allows the characters' personalities and voices to shine through. Use unique word choice, and the use of active rather than passive voice. Make your narrative as true to life as possible.

Give sensory details.
Cover all five senses: taste, smell, touch, sight, and sound. If something is eaten, talk about how it *tastes*. Rather than saying that something is simply "heard," mention how it actually *sounds*.

Expand your vocabulary.
Instead of "pretty," use "gorgeous"; instead of "smelled," use "inhaled"; instead of "hot," use "searing." Vivid words create more vivid pictures.

Use similes and metaphors.
Relate objects or events to other objects or events by using "like" or "as." For example: Instead of saying, "I fell off my skateboard," say instead, "I hit a rock on the sidewalk that caused me to fly up into the air like a rocket." Doing this will allow you to paint a picture in your reader's mind.

Put it all together.
You probably have a draft that is a retelling of events that is fun, expressive, dynamic, and hopefully gripping. As you go over it, rearrange the order, adding emphasis and transitions where needed to build interest and/or suspense that moves the reader along. Remove the random details that lead to nowhere. This will make your writing more cohesive.

Have a beginning, middle and end.
In short, a narrative is a story with a clear introduction, body, and conclusion. Leave your reader with something they can "take away." This should either be a moral or an understanding of a person or way of thinking. They should know YOU better by the end. Deliver this throughout and in your conclusion.

Personal Narrative Writing Rubric

Standard:	Max Points:	Student Score:
Ideas: the main message The writing contains insightful, well-developed commentary (your ideas), which "grow" as the piece develops. Fully articulates the belief; demonstrates original thought and is interesting.	20	
Organization: the internal structure A well-organized introduction or hook; an implied thesis. Contains strong transitions between paragraphs and within each paragraph. Conclusion is clear but leaves the reader to further contemplation.	20	
Voice: the writer's personal style The essay has an engaging & original title; the writer avoids clichés, takes risks, and has a unique imprint on the work. Employs a variety of literary techniques in a skillful manner.	15	
Word Choice: the vocabulary used to convey meaning The writer "shows" not "tells" in the writing. An effective balance of specific, personal, and concrete language along with abstract language.	15	
Sentence Fluency: flow of the sentences Writing contains variety; blend of sentence types. A rhythm to the use of language.	20	
Conventions Proper use of spelling, punctuation, and grammar throughout. Use of language is optimized for an aesthetic effect.	10	

Feedback: **Total Points:** _____

104   Copyrighted material

Additional Templates:

Name: _____

Activity: Journal Writing

Journal Writing

Write your thoughts in free form, meaning whatever comes to mind. Do not worry about censoring or making corrections.

_____

_____

_____

_____

_____

_____

_____

_____

_____

_____

Compare/Contrast

Use the diagram below to illustrate the ways in which two characters are both different and similar. The area that overlaps indicates their similarities.

Directions: Fill in the chart below using several descriptive words and phrases for each character.

Character #1   **Character #2**

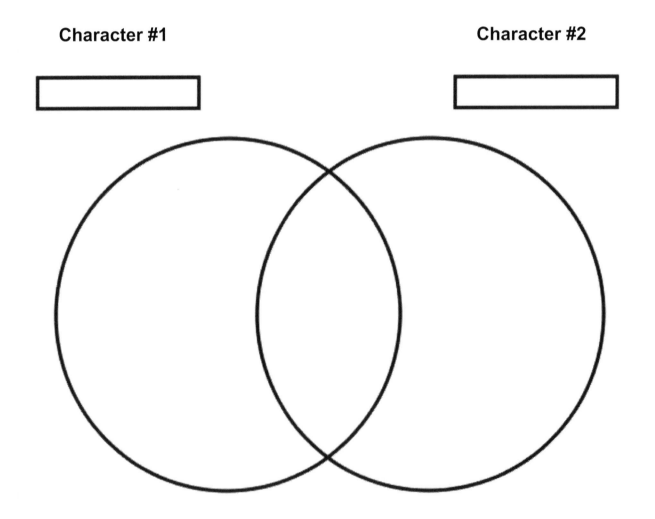

westernmotodrags.com

GO! – Get Creative!

A picture is worth a thousand words. Draw a sketch of any character following the descriptions given in the short story. Feel free to embellish or exaggerate the image as a caricature or cartoon.

Place your drawing in the frame below:

Name: _____   Date: _____

First Read Note Chart

Events/Quotes:	Paragraph:	Observation/Reaction:

Second Read Note Chart

Events/Quotes:	Paragraph:	Observation/Reaction:

You Did It!

Congratulations! You have come to the end of the **Quick Lit Student Workbook** and have completed all of the assignments. You are now officially a **Quick Lit** High School Scholar and can feel confident that you know how to read, interpret, and analyze short fiction in a jiffy. Or, at the very least, you now know your way around an English Literature class like a champ!

Great job!

COURSE COMPLETION
CERTIFICATE

THIS IS AWARDED TO

for successfully completing
The Quick Lit Student
Workbook

JAMIE COLLINS
Author/Teacher

SHAKE SHOCK PRESS
Publisher

Answer Key

Activity #1 - Anticipation Guide: Students' answers will vary. Students are encouraged to journal or discuss any ideas or questions that the topics might evoke.

Activity #2 - First Read (All Levels): Student is to complete the worksheet "First Read Note Chart" adding events, quotes, observations, and/or reactions to the text. Can write directly in the workbook, or print out additional charts from the templates located at the back of the workbook. A minimum of seven entries is required.

Activity #3 – Second Read (All Levels): Student is to complete the worksheet "Second Read Note Chart" adding events, quotes, observations, and/or reactions to the text, paying particular attention to finding use of literary devices. Can write directly in the workbook, or print out additional charts from the templates located at the back of the workbook. A minimum of seven entries is required.

Activity #4 – Pro/Con Chart – Answers will vary.

Activity #5 – Identifying Literary Terms (All Levels): (1) Mood (2) Metaphor (3) Simile (4) Personification (5) Dialect (6) Tone (7) Sensory Detail (8) Dialect (9) Flashback (10) Personification (11) Sensory Detail (12) Colloquialism.

Activity #6 - Short Answer (All Levels): (1) First-person; narrator uses the pronoun "I". (2) Joel – no last name is given. (3) Franklin; the Midwest; references are made to the soil, "crops," "playing in the fields," "dusty roads," and "shallow creeks," bindery work; "city boys" as opposed to the locals; being a "farmer's son." Reference to boarding a train to leave the town/no airport. Most likely this is a very small farm town, perhaps in Southern Illinois or Indiana. (4) The main story takes place in the spring, "Franklin is beautiful, especially in the spring." (5) Thirty years. "It had been thirty long years, yet it felt like yesterday's dream." (6) He was 25. "It was the summer of my twentieth-fifth birthday." (7) Conrad. The narrator was four years old when his brother died. (8) When the narrator was fourteen or fifteen years old, he broke curfew and tried to sneak back to the house. He crept into the kitchen to find his father waiting for him, sitting in the dark, and smoking a cigarette. His father had been drinking as evidenced by the whiskey on his breath. Joel had to wait for his father to finish a second cigarette before he took a strike to the face. [Answers will vary as to what kind of man the father was, including angry, violent, controlling]. (9) The story employs the use of flashback(s). (10) [Answers will vary]. Most likely students will say that they are confused as to why Joel does not interact with his father, but only looks at him from afar. This might make them feel sorrow, guilt, ambivalence, fear, or regret for the narrator and/or for Joel's father.

Activity #7 – Critical Thinking Questions (9-10): (1) [Answers will vary]. The people of the town have blank expressions and show no real emotion caused by years of working in the fields and factories that seemed to have dimmed their spirits. They are but a shell of who they were in a brighter, happier time because of the burden of obligation and hard work. (2) The people of the town believed that the younger generation felt the same obligation that they did to stay on and work the farms and the land; to carry on the traditions that they did and their families before them. Joel knew what was expected of him, but left anyway. He broke tradition. This might have added to a sense of guilt. (3) It might have been easier for Joel to blame someone else for his disillusionment and sadness about his own life, (i.e. the breakup of his marriage). The idea of "becoming" his father was too much to bear. (4) Answers will vary.

Activity #8 – Critical Thinking Questions (11-12): (1) [Answers will vary]. Students might relay that in that moment, the similarities to himself bothered Joel and reinforced his resolve to not become like his father. (2) [Answers will vary]. Students might connect the idea of "accepting" to "weakness" and as justification for Joel to want to break away; to save himself in some way. (3) [Answers will vary]. Students might make the connection to Independence Day as being a victory won over an oppressor; similar to Joel wanting to leave. Ironically, his brother died in battle serving his country. Another connection is that Joel wanted to enlist himself in order to serve his country and to "prove something to himself". (4) Some students might see the statement as being true as evidenced by the fact that Joel does not approach his father at the end, but only looks on at him from afar. Others might argue that he could not avoid going back because the town, his heritage, and guilt, compels him to bring closure to the events in his life that were so significant. The question as to whether or not he gets that closure is left to the reader. [Ideas about remorse will vary].

Activity #9 – Assessment / Writing Prompt (By Grade Level): [Answers will vary]. Refer to Writing Rubric for guidance on scoring.

Activity #10 - First Read (All Levels): Student is to complete the worksheet "First Read Note Chart" adding events, quotes, observations, and/or reactions to the text. Can write directly in the workbook, or print out additional charts from the templates located at the back of the workbook. A minimum of seven entries is required.

Activity #11 – Second Read (All Levels): Student is to complete the worksheet "Second Read Note Chart" adding events, quotes, observations, and/or reactions to the text, paying particular attention to finding use of literary devices. Can write directly in the workbook, or print out additional charts from the templates located at the back of the workbook. A minimum of seven entries is required.

Activity #12 – Characterization Chart (All Levels): (1) Direct. (2) Indirect (thoughts). (3) Indirect (character's speech). (4) Indirect (author is "showing" how the character looks. (5) Indirect. (6) Indirect (the author is "showing" how the character is feeling in that moment. (7) Direct. (8) Indirect (a character's impression(s) of another character).

Activity #13 – Plot Chart (All Levels): (Exposition) – It is morning, and Margaret is washing dishes at the sink after breakfast while her six-month old baby is playing on the floor at her feet with his empty bottle. The screen door is open and construction sounds are heard in the distance as the workers arrive early to work on a project in her yard. **(Rising Action)** – (2) Margaret tries to take the bottle from her son who shrieks in protest. In order to appease him, she removes a ribbon from her hair and slides off her gold ring, places it on the ribbon, and gives it to the boy for him to play with it. Margaret calls to one of the workmen to see if the crewmen want a break; he calls for some ice water and she obliges. (3) When she turns back around, she is surprised to see that another workman is standing in the center of the kitchen. He eludes that she should not have given her son something as dangerous as a ring on a flimsy ribbon. (4) Margaret is obstinate, and questions the stranger's authority to reprimand her. Then, she suddenly looks down to find that her son had the ribbon dangling from his mouth—and the ring is gone. **(Climax)** Margaret screams and launches the boy onto the table, pries his mouth open, searching for the ring, presumably lodged in his throat. She berates herself for being so senseless and stupid. **(Falling Action)** – (6) Once she is certain that the boy was not choking, she bends over him, sobbing and shaking. The stranger looks on still and silent. Margaret can only hear the sound of her heart beating. (7) The stranger begins to speak, telling her that the ring could have fallen on the floor and the boy could have swallowed it. She angrily asks him to leave. (8) The stranger moves across the room, then draws his hand from his pocket and places the ring on the table. Margaret is incredulous to see that he had it all the while. She degrades him. He tells her that he is not sorry for teaching her a lesson and to place the ring back on her hand. **(Conclusion)** – Margaret watches him walk back to the yard. Then, she kisses her son, picks up the ring, and places it back on her finger.

Activity #14 – Literary Terms Quiz (All Levels):
1. C
2. D
3. A
4. B
5. C
6. B
7. A
8. C

Activity #15 – Critical Thinking Questions (9-10): [Answers will vary]. (1) Margaret "frowned at the thought of the dreadful mess they were sure to be making of her yard (par. 4). When she looks out of the window into the backyard she sees her "once plush" lawn and opts to "mourn for her lost tomato garden" at a later time. It is obvious that she does not like disruption and seems to be more comfortable with being in control. This is indirect characterization. (2) When Margaret discovers the stranger, she instantly is on guard. This begins the rising action in which the next series of events will lead toward the climax. The student might note a feeling of tension and suspense beginning to build. (3) Margaret does not want the stranger to perceive that she is frightened and confused and thus, weak. She makes some small talk to seem casual, and to not potentially escalate anything with the man. This might be a strategy or simply a reflex. She "eyes" the kitchen knives in the strainer just in case she would need to defend herself and her son, but the implication is that she might not be certain that she could.

Activity #16 – Critical Thinking Questions (11-12): [Answers will vary]. (1) Students might feel that it is not unusual that Margaret does not immediately pick up her son. Her actions and thoughts at first suggest that she assumes that the man was one of the workers from the yard who was in need of something. She almost scolds him for startling her. Still, she does not seem to trust him. This, might cause some students to wonder why she did not protect her son more readily from any potential threat, especially since the stranger seemed to be a bit "off." (2) With the words, "—and the ring was gone!" the action heightens as Margaret screams and lunges into action, grabbing her son and launching him onto the table. The pacing quickens as he resists, "flailing his arms," and "striking her randomly in the face and chest." She can *feel* her heart lurch. Her inner thoughts reveal her panic and desperation—"STUPID, STUPID mother!" This is in contrast to the next scene in which Margaret then collapses into her son's neck, "sobbing" and begging him to "forgive her." Here, the crisis is abated, and relief replaces the free-falling horror. Pacing the events in this manner brings the reader along on the emotional ride. (3) At this point, Margaret's assessment that the stranger might actually have been reveling in the scene that had unfolded, first confuses her and then—brings her to the brink of anger and fury as when she says, "Shut up!" and "Leave us alone . . . leave us!" At this point, she did not care about his motives, perhaps only finding disdain in her own shortcomings, which was the aim of his little lesson. It stands to reason that she would be mortified and indignant. Her perfect world was shaken.

Activity #17 – Anticipation Guide (All Levels): Students' answers will vary. Students are encouraged to journal or discuss any ideas or questions that the topics might evoke.

Activity #18 – Vocabulary (All Levels): (1) the liturgy of the Eucharist especially in accordance with the traditional Latin rite. (2) a member of a Catholic church; a religious person who believes Jesus is the Christ and who is a member of a Christian denomination. (3) a Christian sacrament in which consecrated bread and wine are consumed as memorials of Christ's death or as symbols for the realization of a spiritual union between Christ and communicant or as the body and blood of Christ. (4) something (such as a cushion or board) to kneel on. (5) a closed, low-cut shoe with one or more straps across the instep. (6) to humiliate or shame, as by injury to one's pride or self-respect. (7) an assembly of persons; a gathering; especially an assembly of persons met for worship and religious instruction. (8) having achieved victory or success; victorious; successful. (9) a long bench with a back, placed in rows in the main part of some churches to seat the congregation. (10) the act of moving along or proceeding in orderly succession or in a formal and ceremonious manner.

Activity #19 - First Read (All Levels): Student is to complete the worksheet "First Read Note Chart" adding events, quotes, observations, and/or reactions to the text. Can write directly in the workbook, or print out additional charts from the templates located at the back of the workbook. A minimum of seven entries is required.

Activity #20 – Second Read (All Levels): Student is to complete the worksheet "Second Read Note Chart" adding events, quotes, observations, and/or reactions to the text, paying particular attention to finding use of literary devices. Can write directly in the workbook, or print out additional charts from the templates located at the back of the workbook. A minimum of seven entries is required.

Activity #21 – Mood Chart (All Levels): (1) Provided. (2) Time had taken its toll on the shoes. Irene is embarrassed to be wearing them (Imagery). (3) Irene is mortified; she is feeling despondent (Tone). (4) Anxiety. Fear. Dread. (Sensory Details and Word Choice).

Activity #22 Short Answer (All Levels): (1) The point of view is third person, limited, as the narrator knows only the thoughts and feelings of a single character. (2) The setting in the interior of a Catholic Church, at a Mass. Irene is seated in a pew. This could be anywhere USA, most likely in May when many First Communion ceremonies were traditionally held in the 1960s -1970s. (3) The main conflict is Irene's predicament with the shoe, which is falling apart by the second. This is an external conflict (man vs. obstacle). Additionally, Irene is struggling with her own regret and shame for being poor. This is an internal conflict of feeling less than the other children around her (man vs. self). (4) "By the time it came around to Irene's turn to wear the shoes, they looked every bit as pitiful as a pair of three-time hand-me-down shoes could look." They were dull and had lost their "magic." The "once bright gold buckle had tarnished" and the "wide strap around the center was frayed and ratted." The "toes turned slightly upward at the tips and were badly scuffed."
(5) The cost of buying a new pair of shoes was not something her family could afford, as "the weekly welfare allotment did not allow for such extravagances as Communion shoes. (7) Answers will vary; possible responses may include: Wealth is not measured by material possessions; inner happiness is priceless; being true to oneself makes one rich in God's eyes.

Activity #23 – Critical Thinking Questions (9-10): (1) She understands that it was not the worn-out shoes that was bothering her; she realizes that it is what they represented—the fact that she was poor. (2) Answers will vary. (3) Answers will vary.

Activity #24 – Critical Thinking Questions (11-12): [Answers will vary]. (1) At first, Irene compares herself to the other children who are dressed nicer and seem to have more money than her. She considers the hand-me-down shoes as a symbol of her poverty that sends the wrong message about who she really is inside. This is evident when the narrator says, "She reasoned that she was not all that different from the others. Everyone laughed and cried and sneezed just the same . . .." (2) Suddenly, "a feeling of relief bathed her broken spirit" and "an idea like magic" came over her, causing her to realize that she was pitying herself when she should have been celebrating her Communion day. This epiphany comes to her "in a glorious instant" suggesting that it might have been the "miracle" that she was seeking. (3) The author describes Irene as advancing to the aisle with her "hands pointed heavenward, her eyes lowered reverently, and her lips pressed into a satisfied smile" as she repeats to herself in affirmation, "What does it matter anyway what a child's got on her feet?" We learn that Irene takes her place in the procession "triumphantly" with a "rich, glad heart" and is fully present as her own authentic self.

Activity #25 – Vocabulary (All Levels): (1) a flaky rich crescent-shaped roll. (2) vitamins, minerals, herbs, or other substances taken orally and meant to correct deficiencies in the diet. (3) the capital raised by a business or corporation through the issue and subscription of shares. (4) a botanical garden devoted to trees. (5) relevant to a subject under consideration. (6) a Japanese dish consisting of small balls or rolls of vinegar-flavored cold cooked rice served with a garnish of raw fish, vegetables, or egg. (7) concerned with beauty or the appreciation of beauty. (8) in a careful or cautious manner. (9) a narrow passageway between or behind buildings. (10) suffering from mange – a mangy animal looks dirty, uncared for or ill.

Activity #26 - First Read (All Levels): Student is to complete the worksheet "First Read Note Chart" adding events, quotes, observations, and/or reactions to the text. Can write directly in the workbook, or print out additional charts from the templates located at the back of the workbook. A minimum of seven entries is required.

Activity #27 – Second Read (All Levels): Student is to complete the worksheet "Second Read Note Chart" adding events, quotes, observations, and/or reactions to the text, paying particular attention to finding use of literary devices. Can write directly in the workbook, or print out additional charts from the templates located at the back of the workbook. A minimum of seven entries is required.

Activity #28 – Identifying Literary Terms (All Levels): (1) Sensory Detail. (2) Simile. (3) Mood. (4) Tone. (5) Onomatopoeia. (6) Satire. (7) Simile. (8) Personification. (9) Imagery. (10) Metaphor. (11) Sensory Detail. (12) Mood.

Activity #29 – Character Traits (All Levels): (1) Provided. (2) Flat – the husband taken at face value has no development or change in the story. (3) Flat—Pierce is non-dimensional and only reacts to his immediate environment as it is presented to him. (4) Flat – we only learn of her reaction to the intrusion on her jewelry counter from the narrator. (5) Flat—the nanny, although she does not protest or object outwardly, is the only presumed constant in Pierce's life. She is only shown taking orders from the Westburys to care for the boy.

Activity #30 – Journal Writing (All Levels): [Answers will vary].

Activity #31 – Short Answer (All Levels): (1) Third person. The reader is given primarily the thoughts and feelings of Catherine, but also in brief, those of her husband as well as Pierce. (2) She most likely works from home; she mentions that her husband "understood little about early behavioral conditioning" and that she was "the psychiatrist in the family," possibly, a child psychologist. She walks "upstairs" at the story's end to "go over some patient files." (3) He speaks to his wife without making eye contact. This is the first clue that he is distant and uninterested in interacting with his family; he taps his coffee cup so that Catherine can summon the kitchen maid to fill it; he is reading *The Wall Street Journal* and discusses financial stocks; he hurriedly leaves for work only waving to his son. He speaks in a formal tone, "You and mother have a grand time," and dashes off importantly. We get the sense that the Westburys are wealthy and/or of a regal class. (4) It is apparent that the couple does not communicate deeply. The husband's first words are a request to Catherine for laundry service. He barely looks at his wife (yet is quick to comment on her looking "frazzled"). Catherine dutifully addresses him sweetly, "Certainly, darling," as she portions out her vitamins. The toddler, Pierce, is propped in front of the TV. They do not seem to be engaged with one another in any real way. (5) She wished on this particular Monday to take him to the arboretum to teach him about trees and flowers, "berries and soil and sand." She is disappointed that the rain has spoiled their plans. Catherine was hoping to give Pierce an experience about nature rather than what he would learn from his flash cards and picture books. (6) On Thursdays, Pierce received his "usual" tutoring sessions in which Catherine would sit with him for an hour and go over flash cards of "famous people" and such. Expecting a baby to recognize and know world figures is a bit of a stretch. The cues given by Catherine (for example, using a disapproving tone for the "Adolph Hitler" flash card) suggest questionable methods. (7) Pierce excitedly frees himself from his mother's grip and jumps directly into the puddle. He does what a toddler would do. He even seems amused with her "disapproving frown." Here, he connects with something that delights and interests him. Catherine tries to turn the opportunity into a lesson as how to spell the word "puddle," but then allows him the pleasure of splashing around in it. [Some students might think that this is out of character for her]. (8) They next visit the gallery downtown. Catherine is careful to lower her voice to impart upon him the weight of the concept of "culture." Of course, he is unable to fully grasp the appeal of it all and instead, drifts to sleep. As evidenced, "The boy yawned widely and rubbed his eyes with the back of his hands, fighting the sleep that the fresh air and walk had induced." (9) When they enter the jewelry store, Pierce "hurried toward the counter," as this was one of his favorite places to visit. He "loved the beautiful diamonds that sparkled in the glass cases." When Pierce thrusts his arms upward to be lifted onto the counter, the saleswoman "fears" for her "precious display." In other words, it is highly unusual for a customer to place a toddler on the glass counter so close to the pricey merchandise. (10) When they arrive home, Catherine hands Pierce over to his nanny for a bath and afternoon nap. Catherine tells him, "You be a good boy. Next Monday, Mother and Pierce will have lots of fun again, okay?" This implies that the outings are a once-a-week occurrence that is scheduled in between Catherine's work and other "duties." Her words are as vapid as the kiss that she almost gives him in the air above his forehead.

Activity #32 – Critical Thinking Questions (9-10): (1) [Answers will vary]. Catherine is fearful of the dog and finds him abhorrent. Still, she tries to turn the event into a teaching moment, and corrects her son by coaxing him to say, *German Shepherd* instead of *Doggie*. (2) Both mother and son are correct, but Catherine's disapproving tone and handling of the situation sends an unintended message to her son, dampening his excitement and ruining the possible milestone of him saying one of his first words for which he receives no praise. The moment is lost on Catherine as she is blind to her own twisted logic. (3) [Answers will vary]. Catherine may or may not have good intentions, however, she is inept when it comes to displaying true maternal instinct or conduct. She treats the boy as if he were a "little man" with total disregard for his needs. It is sad to see how her own lack of attention and approval from her husband manifests itself in her relationship with her son. It is reduced to theories and "going through the motions" of life instead of authentically living it. Of course, one cannot be a mother solely one day a week and mark the task off on a to-do list as "done." Here, the author makes an extreme statement about a different kind of neglect—emotional unavailability in today's world.

Activity #33 – Critical Thinking Questions (11-12): [Answers will vary]. (1) She speaks to him with correctness and platitudes in a sort of superficial way. It is notable that the narrator uses his full name each time he is mentioned, as if this is a point of pride that Catherine takes on, fully attaching herself to what seems to be a lukewarm marriage. The child does not do anything to solve this problem. Catherine seems to be overly accommodating to win her husband's approval, which seems to be difficult to garner. She even expresses inner thoughts of annoyance, as stated, "how dare he say that she looked frazzled these days!" yet, she continues to try to please him by taking youth-enhancing supplements. One gets the impression that she is hungry for her husband's validation. Her over-compensating with her son's "education" reflects this desire to groom her "little man" into his image. (2) Catherine is either oblivious or uncaring about the fact that lifting her son onto the jewelry counter was inappropriate and rather regards the saleswoman's reaction as a "pity" saying that it was "obvious that she had no children of her own." Here, Catherine completely misses the point as to what is and is not appropriate; as if Catherine was an authority on the subject. Her delusion to see herself as entitled and her inability to see herself clearly is ironic. (3) The climax is the actual end of the story when Catherine hands the boy over to the nanny and indicates "Next Monday, Mother and Pierce will have lots of fun again, okay?" Here, it is made known that the day's adventures were a planned, weekly outing designed to be a substitute for an otherwise authentic mother-son bonding opportunity. Just as Catherine strives to achieve perfection and compartmentalization in her own life in response to her shortcomings and disappointments, she treats childrearing with the same clinical approach. This is stunning to the reader in this moment of revelation. One gets the impression that the nanny, "clutching [Pierce] securely to her bosom" is a stark statement on the maternal instinct that Catherine is void of or incapable of exhibiting.

Activity #34 - Anticipation Guide (All Levels): Students' answers will vary. Students are encouraged to journal or discuss any ideas or questions that the topics might evoke.

Activity #35 - First Read (All Levels): Student is to complete the worksheet "First Read Note Chart" adding events, quotes, observations, and/or reactions to the text. Can write directly in the workbook, or print out additional charts from the templates located at the back of the workbook. A minimum of seven entries is required.

Activity #36 – Second Read (All Levels): Student to complete the worksheet "Second Read Note Chart" adding events, quotes, observations, and/or reactions to the text, paying particular attention to finding use of literary devices. Can write directly in the workbook, or print out additional charts from the templates located at the back of the workbook. A minimum of seven entries is required.

Activity #37 – Venn diagram (All Levels): [Answers will vary]. Example: (Differences) Mother is wearing a mink coat to lunch; Lindsay is wearing her parka, scarf, and gloves. (Similarities) Both mother and daughter order an espresso after the meal.

Activity #38 – Characterization Chart (All Levels): [Answers will vary according to passages chosen].

Activity #39 – Short Answer (All Levels): (1) First-person; the story is told by the narrator (Lindsay) and shows her perspective only. Evidenced by the use of "I" as by, "I was really looking forward to meeting Mother for lunch this time, for a change." (2) The narrator is a female; she appears to be a college student in her early twenties; she carries a backpack and is taking some sort of classes. She is meeting her mother for lunch, a "ritual" that seems to be something they do regularly. (3) The restaurant is located "further into the city" where perhaps the narrator lives. The patrons in the restaurant appear to be business-types on their lunch hour and/or closing business deals in the "high-backed chairs" in the upscale restaurant. The location is in a plaza near a high-end shopping mall. This is an urban setting in perhaps near the financial/tourist district of a major city like Chicago or New York. (4) Lindsay is both "teaching" and /or volunteering as well as taking evening classes; it appears that she is working toward a degree in the profession of social work. She laments her mother's disapproval of her "wanting to be something as bourgeois and unglamorous as a social worker." (5) Both mother and daughter order espresso; they both like strong coffee. As stated, "We did agree on one thing, at least." (6) Lindsay knows in that moment that she will have to tell her mother of her plans not to attend Thanksgiving dinner. She knows that this will prove to be particularly upsetting to her mother. "The words spilled from my mouth before I could catch them and rearrange their meaning so they would not be what Mother did not want to hear." (7) Once Lindsay lets out the news that she, her new boyfriend, and friends are planning to go on a ski trip that weekend instead, she feels some relief. She had dreaded the confrontation it would bring. Instead, she says, "For the first time that entire hour, I was finally able to exhale." She felt "unburdened" by the truth that was now laid bare. (8) Lindsay's mother first acts confused, and then pleads her case saying, "I had intended on using the new plates your father brought back from Sapporo last summer," citing her disappointment. She proceeds to pout "like a spoiled child" refusing to be placated. Then, "her eyes turned into a torrent of blue pools," as she asserts, "I should have all my children there, that's all!" (9) The climax occurs when Lindsay reacts and blurts out, "Mother, please!" and "I am not a child, for *God's sake!*" She rises out of her chair, causing a commotion that makes the coffee spill over and reduces the two of them to a "sideshow" of sorts in the restaurant. People start to stare to see what is going on. This is mortifying to Lindsay, which might attest to her otherwise calm and controlled nature. After she quickly apologizes, Lindsay delivers the "crushing truth" across the table in telling her mother, "you've got to stop thinking of life in terms of only what you want." This is a defining moment. (10) Here, her tasting the "bitter brew" is symbolic of Lindsay delivering the "bitter truth" to her mother. The fact that it was "soothing and warm," demonstrates the theme of tough love. It was not with malice that Lindsay tells her mother this truth—it is delivered with love and that makes all the difference.

Activity #40 – Critical Thinking Questions (9-10): [Answers will vary]. (1) Lindsay appears to be a loving and accommodating daughter. She goes out of her way, time and again to appease her mother's wishes. Lindsay has come to accept this about her mother and humors her. This might account for why Lindsay was so nervous about telling her mother about the changes in the Thanksgiving plans. Years of "indulging" her manipulative mother made it all the harder for Lindsay to imagine actually "disappointing" her. It was time for Lindsay to stand up for herself. (2) It is obvious that Lindsay did not find such environments to be her "style" or within her comfort zone. She describes being swept up in "a dizzy frenzy" of corporate types that made her feel out of her element. Her mother chose the location due to its ability to serve gluten free fare and to be situated near a shopping mall. Lindsay typically drank soda and ate French fries; she did not finish her "mediocre" salad. Lindsay had to more-or-less endure the "staged" lunches. (3) Lindsay sees her mother's dramatics as a way to manipulate others. The comparison that she makes to her mother being like a "doll" with "lifeless eyes," suggests that her mother is a shallow and unfeeling person; perhaps incapable of expressing herself in an authentic way. Lindsay's mother shows the world a perfect, polished side of herself, while harboring insecurities and flaws that she works very hard to hide. This fact is not lost on Lindsay who has to navigate carefully past what she knows to be true about her mother.

Activity #41 – Critical Thinking Questions (11-12): [Answers will vary]. (1) While her mother is fashion-conscious and takes pride in "looking chic as ever," Lindsay is more practically dressed in her gym shoes and skirt, wears a parka instead of a mink coat, and has a scarf to ward off the cold instead of a "ridiculous" hat. Their choice in wardrobe, lunch venues, menu choices, differ—as do their outlooks in life. Lindsay affirms, "the contrast of even our very skin only served to magnify the fact." Lindsay's mother is materialistic and socially dependent while Lindsay is grounded and more altruistic in her approach to her career, her life, and her place in the world. It is not realistic for Lindsay's mother to expect the "same things in life" to make them both happy. They are two different people. (2) Because Lindsay has compassion for her mother, she of course, feels "guilty and selfish" at first for blurting out the truth about her mother always thinking of life in terms of only what she wanted. This, leads to a feeling of "liberation" in which Lindsay is able to release all of her resentments that she had been harboring from being under the weight of her mother's oppressive thumb. She was finally free from her mother's "manipulative ploys," "weekly lunches," and "senseless lectures." This is a pivotal moment for Lindsay. She manages in that moment, to claim her *own* wants and needs in spite of the fact that it meant, "disappointing Mother." Rightfully, she then goes on to say, "it would not be the end of the world." (3) This is a very powerful gesture. It is one of love and not selfishness or a desire to cause pain. Lindsay, in this moment sees her mother clearly for the first time—as well as herself. "Maybe a few highlights would do some good." By standing up to her mother, a shift occurs in which the child becomes the parent, so to speak. Both women come to terms with this truth. Lindsay takes back her power and at the same time, expresses great love and respect for the woman who made her who she is, saying, "I don't think that I had ever experienced a moment when I ever loved her more," thus causing the reader to empathize with both characters simultaneously as evoked by this one simple gesture.

Activity #42 – Assessment / Writing Prompt (9-10): [Answers will vary]. Paragraph should follow the general pattern of the model. Paragraph should have a strong topic sentence that reflects the content; should thoroughly compare and contrast the two mothers in a minimum of two examples for each; spelling, capitalization, and punctuation should be correct.

Activity #43 – Assessment / Writing Prompt (11-12): [Answers will vary]. Refer to Writing Rubric for guidance on scoring.

Activity #44 - First Read (All Levels): Student is to complete the worksheet "First Read Note Chart" adding events, quotes, observations, and/or reactions to the text. Can write directly in the workbook, or print out additional charts from the templates located at the back of the workbook. A minimum of seven entries is required.

Activity #45 – Second Read (All Levels): Student to complete the worksheet "Second Read Note Chart" adding events, quotes, observations, and/or reactions to the text, paying particular attention to finding use of literary devices. Can write directly in the workbook, or print out additional charts from the templates located at the back of the workbook. A minimum of seven entries is required.

Activity #46 – Irony Chart (All Levels): (1) Provided. (2) Verbal/Situational. The eldest member of the committee at age eighty-one is indicating that she intends to bid for a date with one of the bachelors, which seems implausible. (3) Dramatic. The reporter is pontificating that the auction is in bad taste and unethical; she vows to expose the committee for their folly in her public column, which the reader is privy to. (4) Situational. The reporter is at first unaware that her movements to exit the row of spectators causes her to be mistaken for a bidder, thus resulting in her unintentionally "winning" the first round of bidding.

Activity #47 – Short Story Quiz (All Levels):
1. A
2. D
3. C
4. B
5. D
6. D
7. D

Activity #48 – Short Answer (All Levels): (1) This story employs the use of alternate point of view combining both third person as well as a first-person narration that switches near the end. The change in POV is indicated by the use of asterisks (***) at the point of the shift. (2) The meeting is being held in a large home of one of the committee members, or in a social center that could hold a "crowd." The mention of Ophelia Macramé "hurrying off to the kitchen" suggests a residence or banquet hall environment. The women are said to be "wealthy widows and divorcees, self-ruling business women" and "wives of Chicago's most influential men," etc. It is likely then, that this meeting is being held in this city. (3) The members of the CUCDY are a collection of the town's most esteemed women, "highly prized for their generous hearts and tendencies toward writing checks with many zeros" for causes dear to their heart. Audrey Winthrop, the chairperson is in the running for a fourth term and leads the meeting with her unorthodox suggestion to hold a bachelor auction. Other women on the committee include, Ophelia Macramé, Constance Peabody, Millicent Donnelley, Hillary McCormick, Camille Rosecrans, Hildegard Watson-Mulberry, and the matriarch, Ramona Cartwright. (4) The business at-hand is the announcement of the committee's participation once again in the annual Wish Makers fund raising drive. The committee's efforts would be to raise money for the Cancer Center of North Shore Children's Hospital to fulfill the wishes of terminally ill children. Audrey proclaims that they can "double" their quota with the decision to hold a bachelor auction. (5) The reporter, who had voted against the idea of having the auction, was vehemently opposed to the concept. "What was being said in defense of human integrity? Human dignity?" She compared the parading of men across the stage to be "bid on" for a date to be demeaning and degrading to all involved. (6) When the reporter had "seen enough," she attempts to exit a row packed with auction attendees. In the process of climbing over "twelve sets of knees to the end of the aisle," her "movements" are mistakenly taken for an indication to increase the bid, whereby she inadvertently "wins" the first round—the purchase of a date with one of the bachelors.

Activity #49 – Critical Thinking Questions (9-10): (1) [Answers will vary]. The narrator refers to the women on the committee as being many of the "community's grandest dames," a term indicating that the women are senior citizens and among the city's older aristocracy. They are further referred to as "respectable women" who are the "backbone of society." Their names are from a by-gone era and their mode of dress seems antiquated and somewhat regal. The type of hors d'oeuvres served at the meeting are upper crust and outdated by today's standards. The mode of Audrey's dress is also a throwback to an earlier time period.

The modern references to the city, the media, and the event, however, suggest that the women are relics of sorts in a modern 20th century world. (2) [Answers will vary]. Students might see the irony of having an auction of this "sort" for the benefit of the Children's Hospital. Others might see it as a more interesting alternative to the crowd funding, festivals, or social media campaigns typically used for raising funds for notable causes today.

Activity #50 – Critical Thinking Questions (11-12): (1) [Answers will vary]. Some responses might include the physical description of Audrey Winthrop as being a large woman, "sporting an impressive jeweled broach at the collar just below her second chin." As well as her "marlin" smile and "exaggerated arches" that "served for eyebrows" that looked like the McDonald's insignia. The references to the ladies growing impatient with Audrey in telling them of her prized idea causes someone to call her out, indicating that the anticipation might cause them all to "die of suspense." When Hildegard Watson-Mulberry objects "vehemently" to the motion, the elder, Ramona Cartwright chimes in with her good vote, saying, "Stay at home then! You can bet I'll be the first in line to start bidding!" (2) [Answers will vary]. Students might see the irony of having an auction of this "sort" for the benefit of the Children's Hospital. Others might see it as a more interesting alternative to the crowd funding, festivals, or social media campaigns typically used for raising funds for notable causes today. Some students might surmise that the author is taking a stand on the concept of exploitation, ageism, and/or reverse discrimination with the objectification of men and/or women. Others might simply see the story as a whimsical account of karma coming around to even the score.

Activity #51 – Get Creative! (All Levels): Alternative Ending for "The Auction" [See Rubric for scoring guidelines]. Sketch/Drawing [Will vary].

Activity #52 - Anticipation Guide: Students' answers will vary. Students are encouraged to journal or discuss any ideas or questions that the topics might evoke.

Activity #53 - First Read (All Levels): Student is to complete the worksheet "First Read Note Chart" adding events, quotes, observations, and/or reactions to the text. Can write directly in the workbook, or print out additional charts from the templates located at the back of the workbook. A minimum of seven entries is required.

Activity #54 – Second Read (All Levels): Student to complete the worksheet "Second Read Note Chart" adding events, quotes, observations, and/or reactions to the text, paying particular attention to finding use of literary devices. Can write directly in the workbook, or print out additional charts from the templates located at the back of the workbook. A minimum of seven entries is required.

Activity #55 – Characterization Chart – Answers will vary. Students should make sure to use actual passages from the text to represent each method for the characters listed.

Activity #56 – Imagery/Sensory Chart – Answers will vary. Students should make sure to use actual passages from the text to represent each sense listed. Examples should conjure the *actual sensations* rather than just mentioning them.

Activity #57 – Conclusions Chart – Answers will vary. Students are encouraged to apply their own thoughts/feelings about each prompt as inspired by the story passages provided. (1) Example: Sometimes in life a missed opportunity can cause great regret, even if it is a simple thing. Larger "missed opportunities" can haunt a person for life, like a vocation never pursued or words of forgiveness never spoken.

Activity #58 - Short Answer (All Levels): (1) First-person; narrator uses the pronoun "I". (2) The narrator is a young political science professor, Dr. Johns, from the United States, who has brought a contingency of students and colleagues to El Salvador. The other people on the trip are: (students) McLadd, Eileen, Michael Anne; (colleagues) Malcolm, and Nathan. The group is there to provide help to the locals; assumingly for a class project on a humanitarian mission that lasts one month. (3) The story opens outside in a barren, "dilapidated" depressed area; the sun is causing a "blasting heat" to descend on "our white American heads." This suggests a foreign locale. The presence of "burnt ash and gunpowder" paints the picture of a war zone. (4) The intense heat mimics the oppression of fear and danger that is present. The author describes the "blasting heat" from the "red-orange sun that sent its fire to cast down" on each of them. The "host of smells" rising from the pavement "mixing with the sweltering heat" conveys a sense of discomfort; the extreme humidity is said to "envelop" the group, turning their skin "moist" and causing their clothes to "cling like wet tissue" to their backs as a result of the town's "hot savage breath." (5) [Answers will vary]. Students might note that the narrative resemble a series of journal entries, written by the narrator in an attempt to chronicle the trip. He is shown "scribbling profusely" in his journal at the breakfast table in Rostia's kitchen. Students may find this structure to be more engaging as they are able to follow the story as a series of vignettes that take place over many days. (6) Here, the narrator sees how the connection is lost on the locals who labor tirelessly to pick the berries from shrubs that resemble something that means something very different to Americans. The idea of "Christmas" has a connotation of celebration and joviality that is not present in their world. The concept of having a "holiday" is one of privilege and freedom. (7) The arrival of the "shipment from the United States" contained schoolbooks and supplies to be distributed to the local children. The narrator was able to experience their reactions, which he says may have served to be the "highlight of the entire journey" for him. (8) The "sad and silent awkwardness" that is hanging in the air is death. Rosita and her family are mourning the loss from early that morning of two of her nephews and a niece, along with "several neighboring children" who had died in an attack on their school. All were under twelve years old. Rosita is crying but silent as she stands alongside her three daughters on the "weather-beaten planks of the porch."

Activity #59 – Critical Thinking Questions (9-10): (1) [Answers will vary]. It is most likely that Rosita and her family took in visitors for lodging. She most likely was desperate for the extra money. She might even have been forced to "house" such guests who came into the country on missionary trips. Her "soulful plea" might have represented her confusion as to why the Americans had even wanted to come, thinking that they could make a difference. She would surely know that they were most likely to leave unfulfilled. (2) The reality of the children's depravity and "desperateness" was not going to be erased by the gifting of school supplies. The look on the face of the young boy near the wagon wheel, whom the narrator never saw again after the church service, was the same look on the "countless faces" around him. Here, the narrator is struck by the gravity of the need and his limitations to fill it. This causes his "once-elated" soul to feel guilt, shame, and regret. He had higher hopes for their mission. (3) Eileen's previous enthusiasm for helping "the Cause" had greatly changed after experiencing first-hand the toll of death and destruction. She might have once had idyllic hopes for "making a difference," but this was crushed in her knowing that they would all leave, return back to the States, and that nothing would change for the people they came there to help. She was broken and disillusioned by the experience.

Activity #60 – Critical Thinking Questions (11-12): (1) [Answers will vary]. The narrator came to El Salvador with a desire to make a difference; to immerse himself in the surroundings and to answer the plight of the people with empathy, compassion, and support. He had come to lead his cohorts on a mission of mercy, and to gather memories and impressions that he could capture in his journal and take back to the States. Some of the experiences he relished as in "Rosita's good breakfast," and the compelling "purity" of Eileen's kindhearted ambitions. Others caused him to question why he had come there, making it difficult for him to sort out the difference between what was real and what was not; as well as the cost, human and otherwise, for the concept of "freedom." (2) The narrator's wistful thoughts about Eileen, signing up for the "Cause" and "wanting to make a difference," are shattered by the "jolt of the distant gunfire." He is aware that the intensity of the climate and the labor were taking a toll on her—on all of them. For this, he is remorseful. The image of the young girl from the church service with her siblings clinging to her with "those wide frightened eyes" haunted him deeply. Eileen's "muffled sobs" cause him to plunge into a deep despair and regret, as he feels personally responsible for bringing her to this place of anguish. He says, "I never felt so far from home," which may also reflect his emotional detachment from his own country, which, in his opinion, was not doing enough to serve the plight. They would all leave having been "changed" significantly from this experience. (3) The narrator wanted to believe that he and his cohorts had come to "do a good thing" and to make a difference. Instead, with Eileen's lament, "And now what, Professor? Back to the land of plenty?" and with "hate rising in her eyes" that once had been filled with light and hope, she cuts him to his heart saying, "I am ashamed." He is certain that the same "wide-eyed faces" of the children haunted her too. He feels that he had failed her in some way; that he has somehow failed all of them. If they had come for answers, there were none to be found. Instead, he carried with him "the burden of one thousand nameless faces," which metaphorically has him forever "looking back," perhaps pouring over his journal entries and photographs, for years afterward in a search for redemption. It is sadly unknown if he would ever find contentment and/or forgiveness within himself for striving for what was most important to him—"to have made a difference."

Activity #61 –Essay Writing Prompt (By Grade Level): Answers will vary. Refer to Personal Narrative Writing Rubric for guidance on scoring.

Resource: Literary Terms

1. **Plot:** The sequence of events in a story; it typically has five elements:
    a) **Exposition:** Introduces setting (time and place), characters, and conflict.
    b) **Rising Action:** Adds complications; conflict becomes clearer; main character is in crisis.
    c) **Climax:** Turning point near/at end of story; the most action, drama, and change happens here.
    d) **Falling Action:** Story slows down and works towards its end; loose ends are being tied up.
    e) **Resolution:** Conflicts are settled; remaining issues are solved (sometimes).

2. **Flashback:** A scene that interrupts the present action to tell what happened earlier.

3. **Foreshadowing:** Hints or clues about what will occur later in the plot through imagery, language, and/or symbolism.

4. **Mood:** The feeling or atmosphere the author creates evoking certain feelings in the reader through words and descriptions.

5. **Setting:** Where and when the story takes place (includes time of day, time period, artifacts/clothing, transportation, etc.). Usually introduced at the beginning of the story.

6. **Dialect:** The way a character speaks if he/she is from a different part of the country; shows the accent and way people talk in a particular region (example: Southern English).

7. **Characterization:** The methods that an author uses to develop the personality of characters, used over the course of a story; there are two types:
    a) **Direct Characterization:** The author tells us directly what the character's personality is like. Example: "Rachael was a bossy little girl prone to tantrums."
    b) **Indirect Characterization:** Information about a character as provided by the author's physical descriptions; the character's speech, thoughts or actions; or other characters' speech, thoughts, or actions. Here, the reader uses his/her own judgment to decide what a character is like.

8. **Character Development:** The way in which a character changes from the beginning to the end of the story—or not.

9. **Trait:** A distinguishing characteristic associated with a particular character (i.e. bravery, folly, arrogance).

10. **Character Types:** There are varying types of characters in fiction that might be defined as any one of the following and/or a combination of such: round, dynamic, flat, static, and/or stock.

11. **Round Character:** Has many character traits; fully developed; usually a main character.

12. **Dynamic Character:** Has a specific experience that causes him/her to change in some way.

13. **Flat Character:** One-dimensional; not fully developed.

14. **Static Character:** Does not change or have any realizations about life; stays the same type of person from beginning to end.

15. **Stock character/stereotype:** Recurring types of characters that fill a particular role; easy to identify (nerd, jock, snob, cheerleader, thug).

16. **Narrator/Speaker:** The person telling the story (not the author). The narrator determines the point of view that the reader will experience.

17. **Protagonist:** The main character; the character we are meant to sympathize with; the character we know the most about.

18. **Antagonist:** The character who is the opposite of the protagonist; he or she causes the conflict for the main character. This could be a villain, for example.

19. **Point of View:** The position from which details in the story are perceived and related to the reader, whose thoughts and feelings the reader has access to. What the character or narrator telling the story can see; his or her perspective. Classified as:
    a) **First-Person:** Story is told by one of the characters in the story; uses "I" internal storyteller.
    b) **Third-Person Omniscient:** The story is told by a narrative voice outside the action who is "all-knowing" and can describe how more than one character is thinking or feeling; the narrator is not a character in the story and is not involved in the action.
    c) **Third Person Limited:** The narrator describes action and dialogue objectively and only reveals the thoughts and feelings of *one* character; the narrator is not a character in the story and not involved in the action.

20. **Tone:** The attitude a writer takes toward a subject; reflects the feelings of the writer (serious, humorous, tragic, suspenseful, angry, ironic).

21. **Conflict:** A struggle between opposing sides or forces; there are two types (external and internal).

22. **External Conflict:** The struggle is between a character and another character, or a character and something non-human and outside of themselves such as a force of nature like a blizzard or flood.

23. **Internal Conflict:** The struggle takes place inside the character's mind; the character has conflicting emotions within themselves often involving a difficult decision. Example: a character's decision to bend his or her morals for a greater good.

24. **Theme:** The main idea in a work of literature. It is a perception about life or human nature that the writer shares with the reader. In most cases, the theme is not directly stated but implied. An example would be "coming of age" or "unrequited love."

25. **Irony:** Twists and surprises in a story; a difference between what is expected and what happens; between what is said and what is meant; between what appears true and what is true. There are three types (verbal, situational, and dramatic).

26. **Verbal Irony:** Saying one thing, but meaning the opposite; sarcasm.

27. **Situational Irony:** The unexpected happens; a sudden twist, for example, at end of the story.

28. **Dramatic Irony:** Audience/reader knows something the characters do not; if the characters had known, they would have done things differently and the outcome of the story would then be different.

29. **Epiphany:** A sudden insight or awareness. (An aha moment).

30. **Figures of Speech:** words/phrases not meant to be taken literary, but are meant to give the reader an image to relate to. Examples may include: metaphors, similes, or slang.

31. **Simile:** A direct comparison between two unlike things using "like" or "as" to make the comparison. Example: Life is like a box of chocolates; you never know what you're going to get.

32. **Metaphor:** A direct comparison between two unlike things. Example: Life is a box of chocolates.

33. **Personification:** Giving human traits to non-human things. Sometimes the sun *smiles*, the wind *whispers*, and the flowers *dance* in the breeze.

34. **Imagery:** Descriptive words or phrases that re-create sensory experiences for the reader by calling forth the use of the senses (sight, sound, smell, taste, and/or touch) whereby creating a picture in the reader's mind.

35. **Allusion:** A direct reference to another literary work or famous person, place or event, such as a mention to a biblical story (Noah's Arc), well-known movie characters, (Dorothy and the Scarecrow), or a reference to a Greek myth, such as, "He is as strong as Hercules."

36. **Symbol:** An image or thing that stands for something else. It can be traditional such as red rose that indicates love, or a sculpture of Einstein that symbolizes genius.

37. **Alliteration:** The repetition of consonant sounds usually at the beginning of words (Porky Pig or Kitty Cat).

38. **Assonance:** The repetition of vowel sounds in close proximity (The **ear**ly **bir**d catches the **wor**m).

39. **Onomatopoeia:** When the word's sound suggests its meaning (*buzz, woof, hiccup*).

40. **Hyperbole:** The use of exaggeration to get a point across. Example: "I am so hungry I could eat a horse."

Made in the USA
Columbia, SC
09 October 2023

24182812R00074